Spelling Success

CLASS 2

Peter Clutterbuck

Blake EDUCATION
Better ways to learn

To Jessie O'Brien

Spelling Success Class 2

Published by Scholastic India Pvt. Ltd.
A-27, Ground Floor, Sigma Centre
Infocity-1, Sector 34, Gurgaon-122001 (India)
Info-in@scholastic.asia

Author: Peter Clutterbuck
Editor: Kerry Davies
Cover and internal design: Janice Bowles
Typesetter: Julian Mole, Post Pre Press.

ISBN: 978-93-5471-905-9
First edition 20210
This reprint edition: June 2024
Printed in India

Contents

Term 1

Term 2

Contents continued

Term 3

Term 4

About using this book

The *Spelling Success* series provides students with learning activities that embrace the different elements of the spelling system. Each book focuses on the different scope and sequences in the development of spelling skills for each age group or skill level.

Book 2 provides students with user-friendly activities to master and develop spelling skills for this year of education. During this year students experience more of the complex ways we form words using letters in a correct sequence. They develop strategies for using sounds and visual patterns to help them strengthen and reinforce their knowledge, building up a comprehensive supply of ready words for written work.

The activities in each book are sequential through the four terms of the school year. This means that it's best to start at the beginning of the Term 1 section and work though to the end, before commencing Term 2 activities, and so on. There are 76 units in this book, 18 per term plus four Review and Test units. Each term is divided into the four areas of knowledge that need to be understood and learned in order to develop a comprehensive mastery of spelling:

Phonological Knowledge — how words sound

Word Function Knowledge — how word function can change spelling

Meaning Knowledge — how context can change word form

Word Fun — puzzles to excite interest in words and spelling

The Phonological Knowledge and the Word Function Knowledge sections include Revision and Test sheets for each term. Four units of Review and Test sheets covering the whole book are provided at the end of Term 4.

This book also contains useful tools to support students with their spelling. At the back of the book you'll find:

★ Useful Words list

★ WINK: Words I Need to Know — space to record problematic words

★ Some Tips for Learning to Spell

★ Assessment checklist

★ Glossary of Terms

Answers to all activities are provided in a special liftout section. A useful **topic list** for the whole year is given before the units.

Spelling Success provides an integrated method of teaching phonics, spelling and vocabulary. These books will improve literacy skills through effective instruction and evaluation based on the latest research into how spelling is best taught and learned successfully.

Book 2 Topic Chart

Long a sound patterns

The letter a can be pronounced as a long a sound, as in **make**, **hay** and **fail**.

A The words in the box all contain the long a sound pattern. Write each word in the correct sentence below. Say each word aloud.

bake **snail** **play** **grapes** **stay** **train**

1. I picked a bunch of ________________.
2. We are going out to ________________.
3. My brother will ________________ us a cake.
4. We must ________________ here until our parents come.
5. We caught the ________________ at the station.
6. I saw a ________________ with a big, black shell.

B Circle the correct word under the picture.

1. 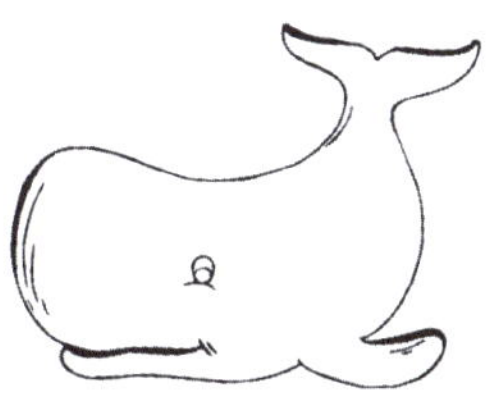 whale fence	**2.**  book nail	**3.**  rain rope
4.  mail bite	**5.**  smile spade	**6.** 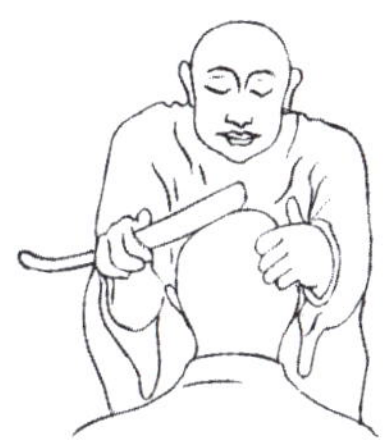 shave shock

Parent/Teacher Signature Date

UNIT 2

Short a sound patterns

The letter a can also be sounded as a short a, as in **bag**, **bat** and **sack**.

A Match each word to its picture. Write the word on the line.

flag **hat** **ant** **axe** **lamb** **rat**

1. 

____

2. 

____

3. 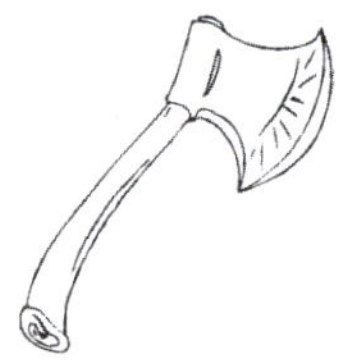

____

4. 

____

5. 

____

6. 

____

B Copy each sentence and choose the correct word from the brackets.

1. A duck can (quack, quick).

____

2. You use a (stump, stamp) to post a letter.

____

3. At the beach you can dig in the (sand, send).

____

4. You have a (handle, candle) on a birthday cake.

____

Parent/Teacher Signature Date

Long e sound patterns

The letter **e** is sometimes pronounced as a long **e**, as in **she** and **seed**.

A Write the correct word from the brackets in the space.

1. Seven days is one ________________. (weed, week)
2. I sleep with a ________________ on my bed. (sheet, shoot)
3. I am sure ________________ will win the race. (he, how)
4. Jack gave it back to ________________. (me, mine)
5. Ella said ________________ would help us soon. (shed, she)
6. I am going to ________________ the kitten I found. (keel, keep)

B Write each word from the box under its correct picture.

beach **teeth** **peel** **bean**

1. 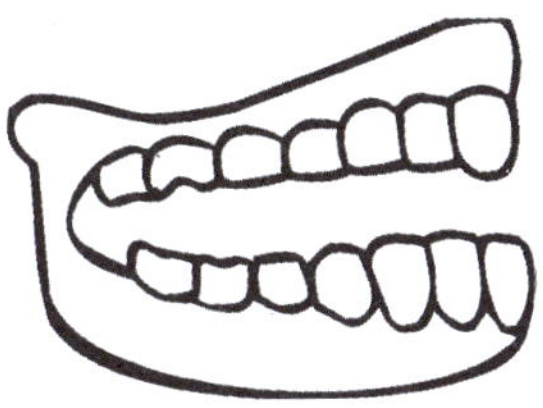 ____________________	**2.**  ____________________
3.  ____________________	**4.**  ____________________

Parent/Teacher Signature Date

UNIT 4

Short e sound patterns

The letter e can also be sounded as a short e, as in **beg** and **pet**.

A Use a word from the box to complete each sentence..

pen	**tent**	**wet**	**cents**	**ten**	**rest**

1. If you are in the rain you might get ________________.
2. I write with a ________________.
3. On the camp we slept in a ________________.
4. We can spend twenty ________________.
5. The number after nine is ________________.
6. After a long walk I like to have a ________________.

B Fill in the blanks in the story below using words from the box instead of the pictures.

bed	**shed**	**dress**	**shell**	**egg**	**nest**

1. One day Sophie got out of 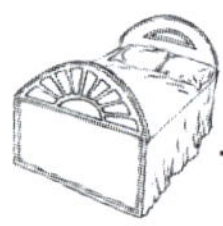 ______________.
2. She put on a blue  ________________ and went out to the
3.  ________________. In a tree she saw a bird's
4. 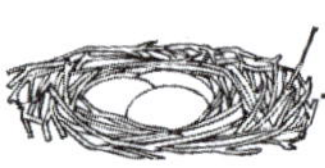 ________________ that had an
5.  ______________ in it. Nearby on the grass she saw
6. a snail that had a large  ______________.

Parent/Teacher Signature Date

Long i sound patterns

The letters **i** and **y** can both make a long **i** sound, as in **lie**, **mine** and **try**.

A Circle the word that matches the picture.

1. 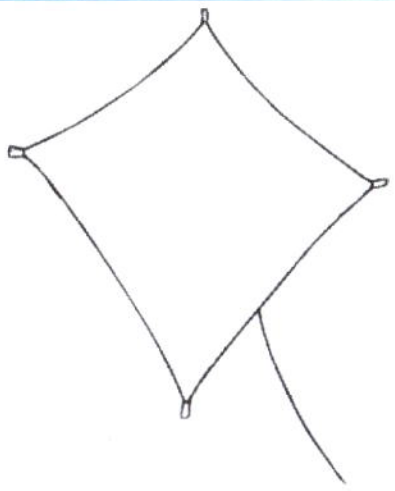 kite line	**2.**  rise five	**3.**  mine mice
4.  pine nice	**5.** 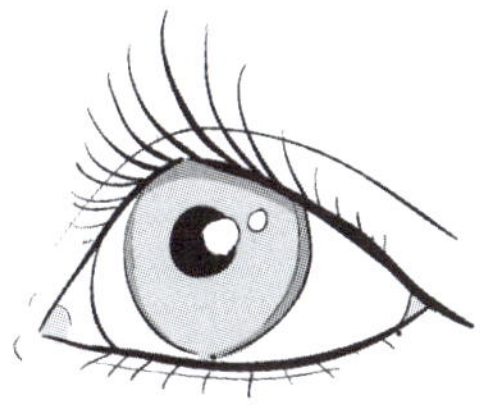 dry eye	**6.**  wipe vine

B Each underlined word below contains the long **i** sound, as in **pine** and **cry**. After each sentence write Yes or No.

1. A bird can fly. ________________
2. We can eat a pie. ________________
3. My age is nine. ________________
4. A savage dog might bite. ________________
5. A blackbird is white. ________________
6. On a hot day the sun will melt ice. ________________

Parent/Teacher Signature   Date

Short i sound patterns

The letter **i** is also often a short **i** sound, as in **bit** and **hit**.

A Write each word under the correct picture.

chin **dish** **swim** **king** **whip** **hill**

1.  ______________	**2.**  ______________	**3.**  ______________
4.  ______________	**5.**  ______________	**6.**  ______________

B Choose the correct word from the brackets and write it in the space.

1. I caught a ________________ in the river. (wish, fish)

2. A ________________ lives in a sty. (fig, pig)

3. The opposite of fat is ________________. (thin, thing)

4. We get ________________ from a cow. (silk, milk)

5. A baby bird is a ________________. (trick, chick)

6. We should always put waste paper in the ________________. (bin, din)

Parent/Teacher Signature Date

Revision

A Write the words in the box under their headings below.

glad	**mat**	**nail**	**flag**
page	**race**	**hat**	**stay**

Long a words (as in **skate** and **pail**)

Short a words (as in **cat** and **axe**)

____________ ____________ ____________ ____________

____________ ____________ ____________ ____________

B Write the words in the box under their headings below.

me	**cent**	**wet**	**week**
best	**she**	**keep**	**tent**

Long e words (as in **meet** and **he**)

Short e words (as in **beg** and **ten**)

____________ ____________ ____________ ____________

____________ ____________ ____________ ____________

C Write the words in the box under their headings below.

win	**list**	**kite**	**thick**
nice	**sky**	**chip**	**fire**

Long i words (as in **pine** and **my**)

Short i words (as in **bit** and **tick**)

____________ ____________ ____________ ____________

____________ ____________ ____________ ____________

Parent/Teacher Signature Date

Test 1

Choose the correct word in the brackets and write it in the space.

1	I saw a (snail, snale) in the garden.	1
2	It might (rane, rain) this afternoon.	2
3	I used a (stamp, stamf) to post the letter.	3
4	I heard the duck (quak, quack).	4
5	I put the tools in the garden (shead, shed).	5
6	I pulled the (weed, wede) out of the garden.	6
7	We slept in a (tennt, tent) last night.	7
8	I found an (eg, egg) on the grass.	8
9	I tried to fly my (kyte, kite).	9
10	He has a sore (eye, eyy).	10
11	I saw a (fish, fysh) in the water.	11
12	The (chik, chick) stayed close to the hen.	12

Total correct ______
12

Parent/Teacher Signature Date

Test 2

The underlined words are spelled wrongly. Write each one correctly in the space.

1	We must <u>staye</u> here until 5 o'clock.	1
2	I hammered the <u>nale</u> into the wood.	2
3	I chopped the wood with an <u>ax</u>.	3
4	The <u>candel</u> was burning brightly.	4
5	Next <u>weke</u> I am going to the disco.	5
6	My mother said I could <u>kepe</u> the kitten.	6
7	The snail has a large <u>shal</u>.	7
8	I had twenty <u>sents</u> to spend.	8
9	I ate a <u>pye</u> for lunch.	9
10	We saw the cat chasing the <u>mise</u>.	10
11	We got a bottle of <u>milc</u> to drink.	11
12	We went for a <u>swimm</u> in the water.	12

Total correct ______ / 12

Parent/Teacher Signature   Date

UNIT 10

Plurals, adding s

Plural means more than one. To make the plural of many words, you just add an **s**.

Add an **s** to each word to make each word mean more than one. The first one has been done for you.

1.

one cat two *cats*

2.

one bike two ________________

3.

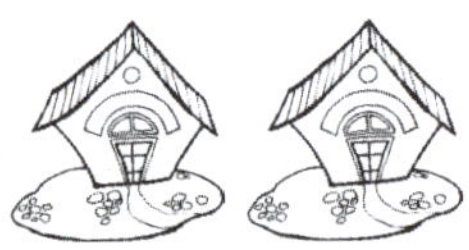

one house two ________________

4.

one chair three ________________

5.

one hen three ________________

6.

one table three ________________

7.

one ball four ________________

8.

one cow two ________________

Parent/Teacher Signature Date

Plurals, words ending in sh and ch

To make plurals for words that end in sh and ch you need to add es. Examples: one arch, two arches; one crash, four crashes

Add es to make each word mean more than one. The first one has been done for you.

1.

one peach two peaches

5.

one watch three ________________

2.

one bush four ________________

6.

one dish two ________________

3.

one brush two ________________

7.

one witch two ________________

4.

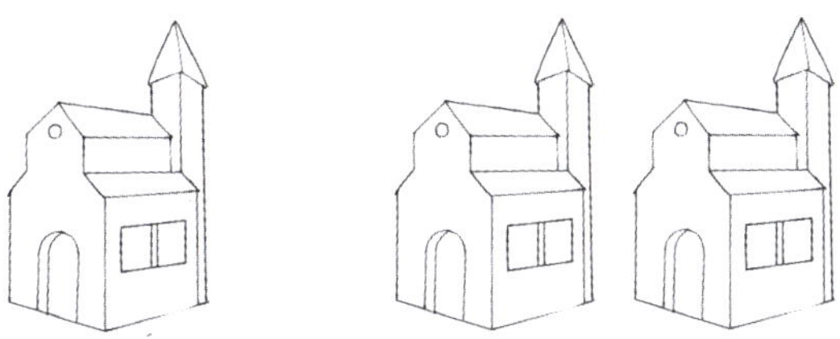

one church two ________________

8.

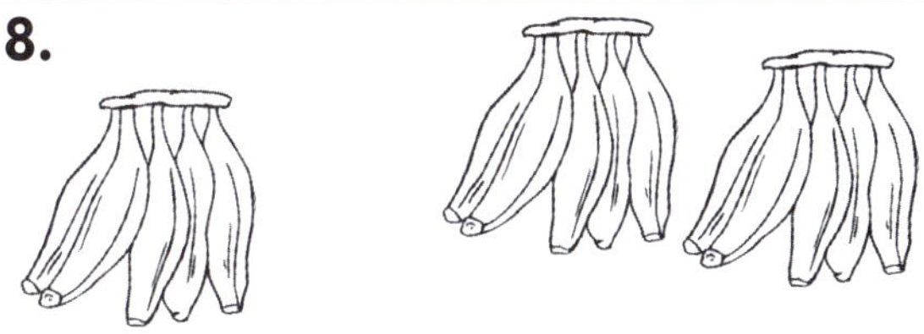

one bunch two ________________

Parent/Teacher Signature Date

Plurals, words ending in s, ss and x

To make the plural of words that end in **s**, **ss** and **x** you add **es**. Examples: one gas, two gases; one class, many classes; one fox, three foxes

A Add **es** to the end of each word to make its plural.

1.

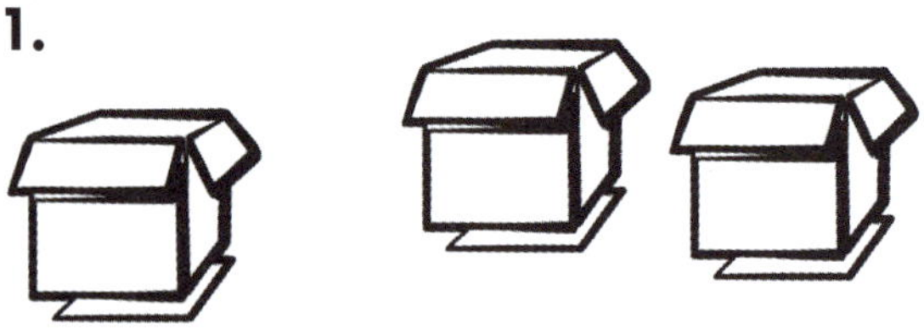

one box two ______________

4.

one fox three ______________

2.

one bus two ______________

5.

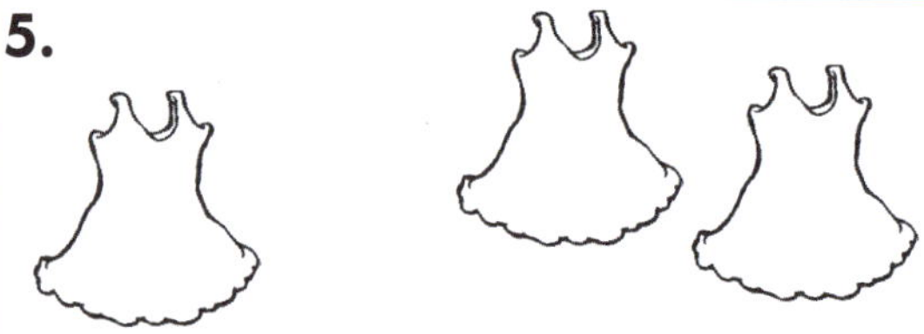

one dress two ______________

3.

one glass three ______________

6.

one kiss three ______________

B Add **es** to each word in brackets and write it in the space.

1. I had three ______________ before I got the correct answer. (guess)
2. The snake made several ______________ to keep us away. (hiss)
3. My school has fifteen ______________. (class)
4. My father has three ______________ at work. (boss)

Parent/Teacher Signature Date

Plurals, words ending in y and words that change

A Words that end in **y** with a vowel before it simply add **s** to make their plural (one day, seven days). Write the plural of each word by adding **s**.

1.

one boy two ____________

4.

one monkey three ____________

2.

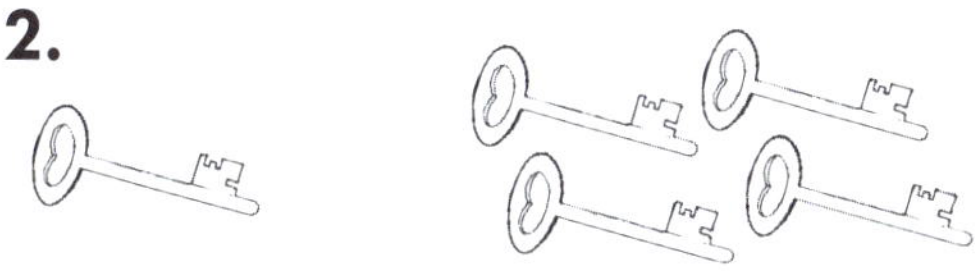

one key four ____________

5.

one donkey two ____________

3.

one turkey two ____________

6.

one toy many ____________

B To make their plurals some words change completely (one woman, two women). Can you think of the plural for these words? Write each one in the box.

1.

one mouse lots of ____________

3.

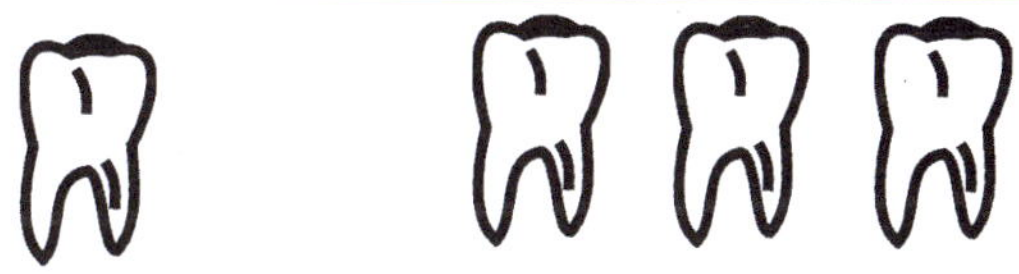

one tooth three ____________

2.

one man three ____________

4.

one child two ____________

Parent/Teacher Signature Date

Revision

A Some words in the box are singular (one) and some are plural (more than one). Write the words under the headings.

boxes	bunch	matches	church
dish	tables	monkey	mice
guesses	desk	turkeys	book
dress	donkeys	box	teeth

Singular		Plural	
____	____	____	____
____	____	____	____
____	____	____	____
____	____	____	____

B To change some of the words in the box into plurals you need to add **s**, for some you need to add **es** and for some you need to change the word completely. Write the words under their headings below.

bush	tree	glove	man
mouse	witch	box	ditch
day	foot	goose	circle

+ s (bird, birds)	+ es (church, churches)	Word change (louse, lice)
____	____	____
____	____	____
____	____	____
____	____	____

Parent/Teacher Signature Date

Test

The underlined words are spelled wrongly. Write each correctly in the space.

1	I saw two catts drinking milk.	1
2	We moved all the tabels across the room.	2
3	The four birdes flew out of the nests.	3
4	I ate two juicy peachs for lunch.	4
5	I helped my father do the dishs.	5
6	There are lots of bushs in our garden.	6
7	There were two busses in the parking lot.	7
8	Lily has three dresss to wear.	8
9	I opened the doors with the set of keyes.	9
10	My little brother has lots of toyes.	10
11	There were lots of mouses in the barn.	11
12	Sam had to have two tooths taken out.	12

Total correct ________ / 12

Parent/Teacher Signature Date

UNIT 16

Compound words 1

Compound words are made up of two or more words. Examples: cross + road = crossroad; grape + fruit = grapefruit

A Choose the correct word to complete each compound word. Write it in the space.

noon chair  **1.** arm________	cup spoon  **4.** egg________	bird clock  **7.** black________
fish moon 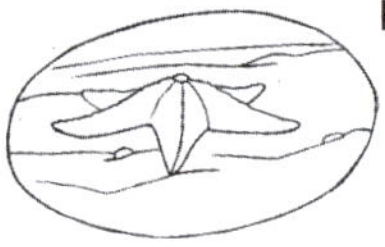 **2.** star________	dog fly  **5.** butter________	lace bird  **8.** shoe________
set fall  **3.** water________	smith ball  **6.** foot________	hopper book 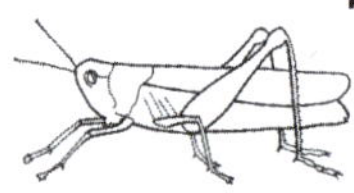 **9.** grass________

B Use a compound word from the box to complete each sentence.

pancakes	**bathroom**	**bulldog**
snowflake	**birthday**	**afternoon**

1. I took a shower in the ________________.
2. The ________________ bit the boy on the leg.
3. We went swimming in the ________________.
4. Tomorrow is my tenth ________________.
5. The hot sun melted the ________________.
6. Dad makes ________________ on Sundays.

Parent/Teacher Signature Date

Compound words 2

Compound words are made up of two or more words. Examples: cross + road = crossroad; grape + fruit = grapefruit

A Choose a word from the box to complete each compound word.

lace **paste** **shoe** **side** **fish** **bow**

1.  gold____________	**2.**  rain____________	**3.** 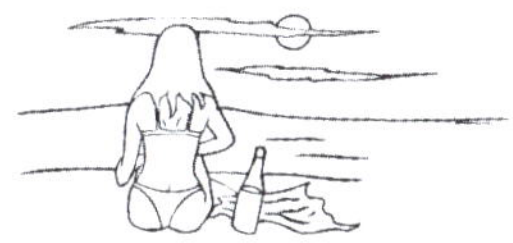 sea____________
4. 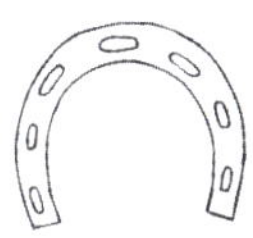 horse____________	**5.** 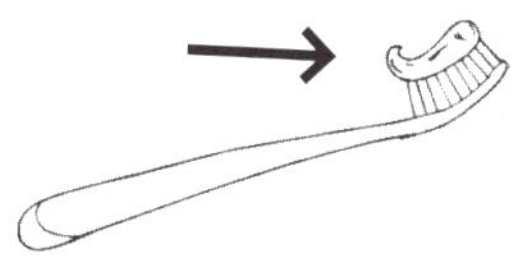 tooth____________	**6.** 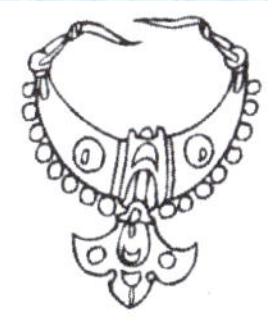 neck____________

B Add a word from List B to a word in List A and write the compound word. Then draw a picture to match the word.

List A	space	straw	grass	news	bath	wind
List B	room	paper	ship	berry	mill	hopper

1. ____________	**2.** ____________	**3.** ____________
4. ____________	**5.** ____________	**6.** ____________

Parent/Teacher Signature Date

UNIT 18

Crosswords

Copy the words in the boxes below into the crosswords. Use one letter for each space. Two words of the first crossword have been filled in for you.

1. b		2.
u	■	
3. g	u	n

1.		2.
	■	
3.		

A gun bat ten bug

B rat cap car pot

1.		2.
	■	
3.		

1.		2.
	■	
3.		

C cow wig cat tug

D tap fan fat nap

Parent/Teacher Signature Date

Long o sound patterns

The letter **o** is sometimes pronounced as a long **o** sound, as in **rope**, **soap** and **flow**.

A Write each word from the box under its correct picture.

loaf **smoke** **bone** **rose** **soap** **nose**

1.  ______________	2. 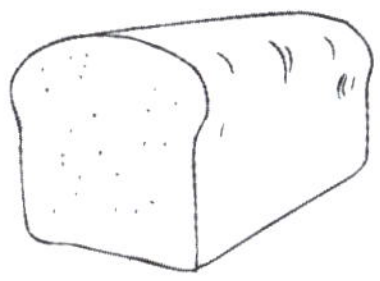 ______________	3. 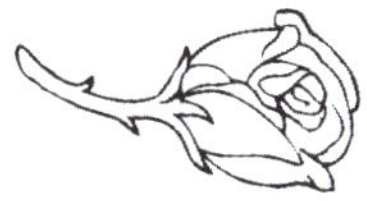 ______________
4.  ______________	5.  ______________	6.  ______________

B Fill in the blanks in the story below using the words from the box instead of the pictures.

smoke **toe** **rope** **home** **nose** **hose**

1. One day a boy tied a  ______________ around
2. his  ______________. When the boy woke
3. he saw some 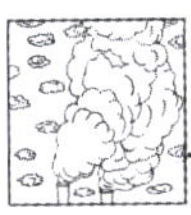 ______________ and he could
4. smell it with his  ______________. He grabbed a
5.  ______________ and ran to his friend's
6.  ______________ to make sure he was safe.

Parent/Teacher Signature Date

UNIT 20

Short o sound patterns

The letter **o** can also make a short **o** sound, as in **hop** and **got**.

A Write each word from the box under its picture.

fox	lollipop	rod	clock	lock	sock

1.  ______________	**2.**  ______________	**3.** 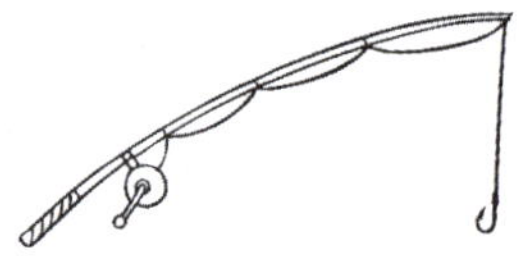 ______________
4.  ______________	**5.** 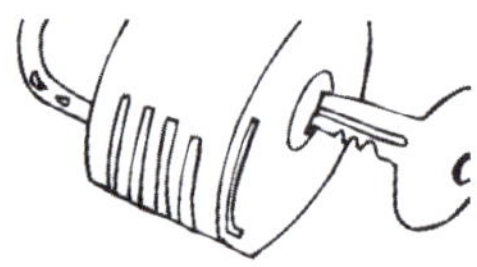 ______________	**6.**  ______________

B The underlined words all have a short **o** sound. Read each sentence. After each one write Yes or No.

1. You can chop wood with an axe. ______________
2. A dog can bark. ______________
3. A moth has two wheels. ______________
4. A car must stop at a green traffic light. ______________
5. We can buy things at a shop. ______________
6. A frog can hop. ______________

Parent/Teacher Signature Date

Long u sound patterns

The letter **u** can be sounded as a long **u**, as in **fuse** and **bugle**.

A Use a word to fill the spaces in each sentence.

cute	**tune**	**cube**
pure	**fume**	**cure**

1. The ______________ white snow started to melt.
2. I put the ice ______________ in my drink.
3. Olivia played a ______________ on the piano.
4. The new puppy was very ______________.
5. Mum was so angry she began to ______________.
6. The doctors are trying to find a ______________.

B The underlined words each contain a long **u** sound. Write Yes or No after each sentence.

1. If something is tiny it is huge. ______________
2. You can buy glue in a tube. ______________
3. A mule is an animal like a donkey. ______________
4. You can eat a student. ______________
5. A bugle is played on a keyboard. ______________
6. Spiders are really cute. ______________

Parent/Teacher Signature   Date

UNIT 22

Short u sound patterns

The letter u can also make a short u sound, as in **cut** and **thrust**.

A Write each word from the box under its picture.

hut **bug** **bus** **gun** **truck** **trunk**

1.
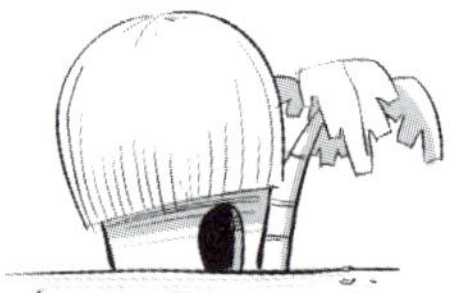
____

2.

____

3.
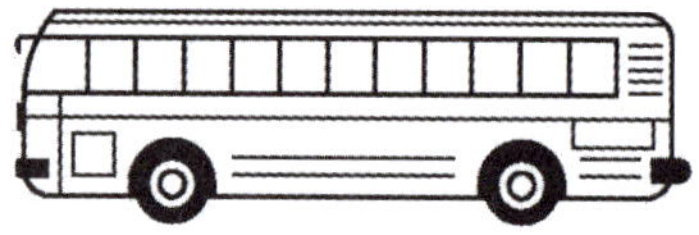
____

4.
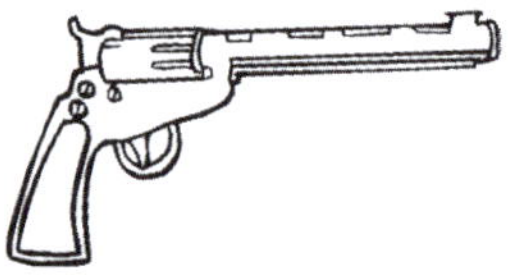
____

5.

____

6.
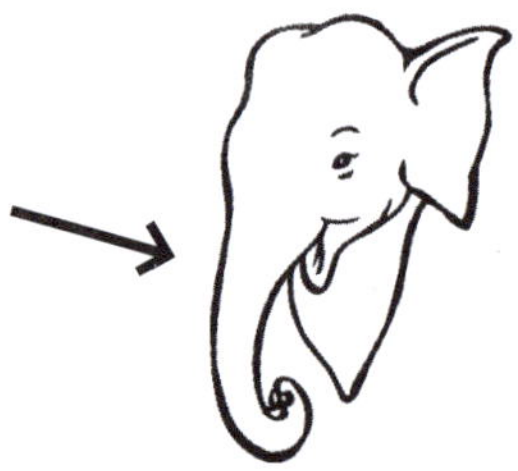
____

B Use the words in the box to fill in the blanks in this story.

jug **bun** **plum** **cup**

1. One day a girl took a  _______________ and
2. a  _______________ to put on the kitchen
3. table near a  _______________ that she filled
4. with milk from the  _______________.

Parent/Teacher Signature Date

r-Influenced vowels, ar

When the letter **a** is followed by an **r**, the **a** is pronounced like a long **ar** sound, as in **car** and **card**.

A Join the word pieces and write the word on the line. Then draw a picture to match the word.

1. st + ar ______	**2.** far + m ______	**3.** gar + den ______
4. car + d ______	**5.** shar + k ______	**6.** par + k ______

B Choose the correct word in the brackets. Write it in the space.

1. We put (carpet, market) ______________ on the floor.
2. A person has two (harms, arms) ______________.
3. An angry dog will (hard, bark) ______________.
4. At night it becomes (dark, stark) ______________.
5. A rock can be very (farm, hard) ______________.
6. A (shark, park) ______________ is a very large fish.

Parent/Teacher Signature Date

r-Influenced vowels, er sound

When the letter e is followed by an r, the e is pronounced as a long er sound, as in **her** and **butter**. The er sound is also made by the letters ir and ur, as in **girl**, and **turn**, and sometimes by the letters or, as in **work** and **word**.

A Join the word pieces and write the word on the line. Then draw a picture to match the word.

1. bir + d ______	**2.** wor + m ______	**3.** per + son ______
4. tur + tle ______	**5.** danc + er ______	**6.** cir + cle ______

B Use a word from the box to complete the sentences below.

circus **perch** **verse** **surf** **birthday** **fern**

1. Part of a poem is a ______________.
2. A parrot sits on a ______________.
3. In summer I love to swim in the ______________.
4. A ______________ is a kind of plant.
5. We are having a ______________ party next week.
6. I saw a clown at the ______________.

Parent/Teacher Signature Date

Revision

A Write the words in the box under their headings below.

stone	clock	boat	lock
stop	home	shop	woke

Long o sound (bone) Short o sound (hop)

_______________ _______________ _______________ _______________

_______________ _______________ _______________ _______________

B Write the words in the box under their headings below.

huge	crust	cure	luck
lump	tube	plum	pure

Long u sound (cube) Short u sound (cut)

_______________ _______________ _______________ _______________

_______________ _______________ _______________ _______________

C Add **ar** or **er** in the space. Write the words under their headings below.

c___d	h___b	b___k	g___m
h___	st___	f___n	___m

ar er

_______________ _______________ _______________ _______________

_______________ _______________ _______________ _______________

Parent/Teacher Signature Date

Test 1

The underlined word is spelled wrongly. Write it correctly in the space.

1	I bought a louf of bread at the shop.	1
2	The dog buried a bowne in the yard.	2
3	The hands of the cluck show ten o'clock.	3
4	I pulled my sok onto my left foot.	4
5	The fluffy cat was very cuet.	5
6	A mouse is tiny but an elephant is hewge.	6
7	At the farm we saw lots of dacks.	7
8	My father drives a large treck to Sydney.	8
9	I sent a birthday kard to my friend.	9
10	At the ocean I saw a large sharrk.	10
11	I like to going to the cercus.	11
12	That furn is bright green.	12

Total correct ______
12

Parent/Teacher Signature Date

Test 2

Choose the correct spelling of the word in brackets.
Write the correct word in the space.

1	We washed our faces with (sope, soap).	1
2	We saw (smoke, smock) from the fire.	2
3	I always (lok, lock) the door.	3
4	There was a (mowth, moth) on the leaf.	4
5	They said his heart was (puwer, pure).	5
6	The new (student, stewdent) tried very hard.	6
7	A large (truk, truck) carried the furniture.	7
8	An elephant has a long (trunk, trank).	8
9	I picked some flowers in the (gardin, garden).	9
10	We went for a picnic in the (parrk, park).	10
11	I did not know what (shirt, shert) to wear.	11
12	This is the second (tirm, term) of the year.	12

Total correct ______
12

Parent/Teacher Signature Date

UNIT 28

Short and long words

The letters of the alphabet are used to make words. Some words are short, having only two or three letters, such as **if**, **and**, **no** and **hat**. Some words are long and have many letters, such as **beautiful**, **bananas** and **television**. Words that are medium are in between, such as **forget**, **learn** and **become**.

A Some of the words in the box are long words and some are short words. Copy them under the headings below.

in	kangaroo	elephant	holidays	the	of
cupboard	helicopter	aeroplane	cat	is	sit

Short words **Long words**

_______________ _______________ _______________ _______________

_______________ _______________ _______________ _______________

_______________ _______________ _______________ _______________

B When we write, we have to leave a space between each word.

This is incorrect: Acatcanrun.

This is correct: A cat can run.

Write the words and leave a space between each one.

1. Abirdcanfly. ____________________
2. Mycatisblack. ____________________
3. Wewentonaship. ____________________

Parent/Teacher Signature Date

UNIT 29

Adding ed, no change

When you add **ed** to some words you change how you use the word but the spelling of the base word does not change.
Example: Today I bake. Yesterday I baked.

A Add **ed** to the words in brackets and write the word in the space. Draw a picture for each one.

1.	**2.**	**3.**
The kangaroo ______________ the fence. (jump)	Riley ______________ his face. (wash)	We ______________ in the yard. (play)
4.	**5.**	**6.**
Ruby ______________ the pram. (push)	The ship ______________ across the sea. (sail)	Dad ______________ us tea. (cook)

B Make the word in brackets end in **ed**. Write the word on the line.

1. We ______________ our teacher tidy the room. (help)
2. I ______________ my dog to get a bone. (call)
3. The car ______________ onto the freeway. (turn)
4. The toddler ______________ across the room. (crawl)
5. We ______________ in a motel last night. (stay)
6. We ______________ everywhere for the lost book. (look)

Parent/Teacher Signature   Date

UNIT 30

Adding ing, no change

When you add **ing** to some words you change how you use the word but the spelling of the base word does not change.
Example: I will call you tomorrow.
I am calling you right now.

A Look at each picture below. Add **ing** to the word in brackets and write it in the space.

1.  Ethan is ______________ some food. (cook)	**2.**  The children are ______________ to read. (learn)	**3.**  Talia is ______________ her dog. (call)
4.  The yacht is ______________ across the lake. (sail)	**5.**  Jack is ______________ the pram. (push)	**6.**  Jade is ______________ the lawn. (mow)

B Make the word in brackets end in **ing**. Write the word in the space.

1. The cat is ______________ the fence. (jump)
2. The children are ______________ in the yard. (play)
3. Mike is ______________ in the bed. (sleep)
4. The baby is ______________ across the room. (crawl)
5. She is ______________ the pancakes over. (turn)
6. We are ______________ the teacher. (help)

Parent/Teacher Signature Date

Adding ed or ing, doubling letters

For words that end in a short vowel and a consonant you double the last letter before adding ed or ing.
Examples: I pat the dog. I patted the dog.
I am patting the dog.

A Make the word in brackets end in ed. Don't forget to double the last letter. Draw a picture of each one.

1.	2.	3.
Riley __________ the wood. (chop)	Jack __________ the floor. (mop)	Sophie __________ the ball. (drop)
4.	**5.**	**6.**
The frog __________ over the lawn. (hop)	Mia __________ across the yard. (skip)	Tom __________ the dog. (pat)

B Make the word in brackets end in ing. Write it in the space.

1. The car is __________________ at the corner. (stop)
2. The dog is __________________ its tail. (wag)
3. William is __________________ over the rope. (trip)
4. Oliver is __________________ my leg for me. (rub)
5. The dog is __________________ the bone in its teeth. (grab)
6. The boy is __________________ over on the ice. (slip)

Parent/Teacher Signature Date

Revision

A Write the words in the box under their headings below.

driver	but	house	beautiful
aeroplane	sailor	hippopotamus	hit
and	helicopter	if	table

Short words		Medium words		Long words	
______	______	______	______	______	______
______	______	______	______	______	______

B Make the words in the box end in **ed** and write them under their headings below.

wait	stop	hop	pass
wag	jump	play	drag

+ ed (box, boxed)		Double last letter + ed (skip, skipped)	
______	______	______	______
______	______	______	______
______	______	______	______

C Add **ing** to these words and write them in a sentence.

1. play ______________________________
2. stop ______________________________
3. help ______________________________

Parent/Teacher Signature Date

Test

Choose the correct spelling of the word in brackets.
Write your answer in the space.

1	The kangaroo (jumpt, jumped) the fence.	1
2	Sally (cooked, cookt) the food.	2
3	The boat (sailed, saild) across the lake.	3
4	I (helpt, helped) my mother clean the room.	4
5	Isabelle (chopped, choppt) the wood.	5
6	The clumsy boy (droped, dropped) the glass.	6
7	Tom (patted, pated) the dog.	7
8	Olivia (rubbed, rubed) her sore leg.	8
9	The children are (learning, learnen) how to read.	9
10	Joshua is (callen, calling) his dog.	10
11	We are (cooken, cooking) some food.	11
12	Oliver is (sleepping, sleeping) in his bed.	12

Total correct ______
12

Parent/Teacher Signature   Date

UNIT 34

Homophones 1

Homophones are words that sound the same but have different spellings and different meanings.
Example: bear (animal), bare (naked)

A Circle the correct word for each picture. Write the word on the line.

1.	2.	3.
____________  four for	____________  sun son	____________  sale sail
4. ____________  tale tail	**5.** ____________ 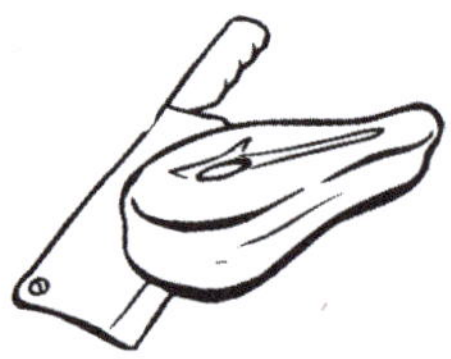 meat meet	**6.** ____________  male mail

B Choose the correct word to complete each sentence.

1. Mia and I went ____________ the disco last night. (two, to)
2. We will ____________ for lunch. (meet, meat)
3. Last ____________ we went to the zoo. (week, weak)
4. The cat bit the dog on the ____________. (tale, tail)
5. I will ____________ a present for my mother. (by, buy)
6. Bill ____________ all the answers. (knew, new)

Parent/Teacher Signature   Date

Homophones 2

Homophones are words that sound the same but have different spellings and different meanings.
Example: week (seven days), weak (not strong)

A In each box draw a picture for the circled word.

1. won (one)	**2.** would (wood)	**3.** flour (flower)
4. to (two)	**5.** see (sea)	**6.** bare (bear)

B Circle the correct word.

1. The (be, bee) stung her on the foot.
2. I (saw, soar) my friend at school.
3. The car raced along the (rode, road).
4. I ate a juicy (pair, pear) for lunch.
5. The girls (ate, eight) all the lollies.
6. I tied a (not, knot) in the string.

Parent/Teacher Signature Date

UNIT 36

Word grids

A In the letters in the grid, find and circle the word that matches the picture. Write the words on the lines.

s	h	i	p
t	e	g	g
a	p	i	g
r	s	u	n

1. ____________ 
2. ____________ 
3. ____________ 
4. ____________ 
5. ____________ 

B In the letters in the grid, find and circle the word that matches the picture. Write the words on the lines.

t	g	r	g
r	a	i	o
e	t	n	l
e	e	g	d
b	i	r	d

1. ____________ 
2. ____________ 
3. ____________ 
4. ____________ 
5. ____________ 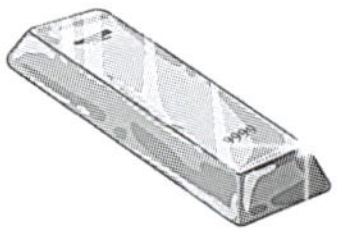

Parent/Teacher Signature Date

Sound patterns, long and short oo

The letters **oo** together can be pronounced as a long **oo** sound, as in **room** or they can be a short **oo** sound, as in **look**.

A Sort the words beneath the pictures under the headings below.

 book	 boot	 moon	 hook
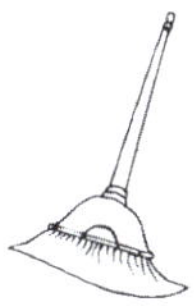 broom	 foot	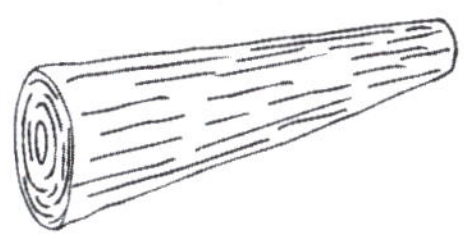 wood	 school

Long oo sound (room)		**Short oo sound (look)**	
______	______	______	______
______	______	______	______

B Circle the word that matches the picture.

1.  brook, soot	**2.**  hood, good	**3.** 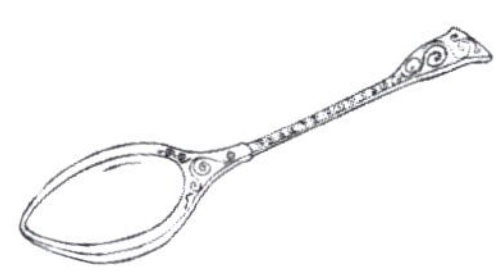 broom, spoon

Parent/Teacher Signature Date

UNIT 38

Sound patterns, ai

The letters **ai** together are pronounced as a long **a** sound, as in **rail** and **fail**.

A Write each word from the box beneath its picture.

rain **paint** **train** **snail** **mail** **tail**

1.

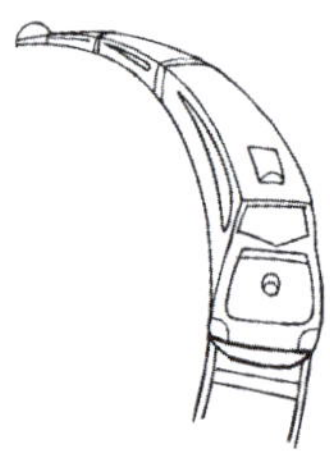

____

2.

____

3.

____

4.

____

5.

____

6.

____

B After each sentence write Yes or No.

1. If glue gets on your clothes it will stain them. ________________
2. If you are frail you are very strong. ________________
3. Your brain helps you think. ________________
4. You might find a sail on a yacht. ________________

Parent/Teacher Signature Date

Sound patterns, oa

The letters **oa** together are pronounced as a long **o** sound, as in **oats**.

A Write each word from the box beneath its picture below.

boat **goat** **road** **coat** **loaf** **soap**

1.  ______________	**2.**  ______________	**3.**  ______________
4.  ______________	**5.** 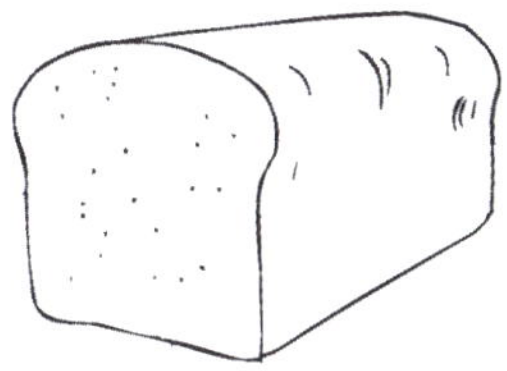 ______________	**6.** 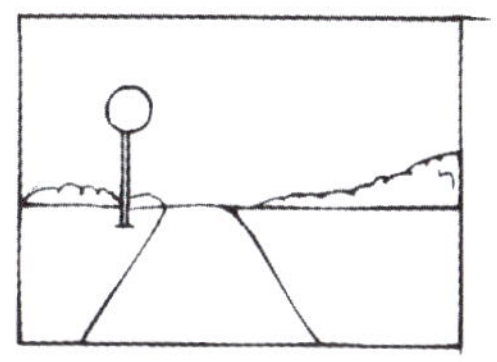 ______________

B The underlined words all contain the letters **oa**. After each sentence write Yes or No.

1. Cork will float in water. ______________
2. A car can go along a road. ______________
3. A frog can croak. ______________
4. A dog likes to eat oats. ______________
5. You can eat toast for breakfast. ______________
6. A camel can carry a heavy load. ______________

Parent/Teacher Signature Date

Sound patterns, oi and oy

The letters oi together are pronounced as in **toil** and **soil**. The letters oy also make an oi sound, as in **joy** and **coy**.

A Draw a line from the word to the picture.

coin boil coil

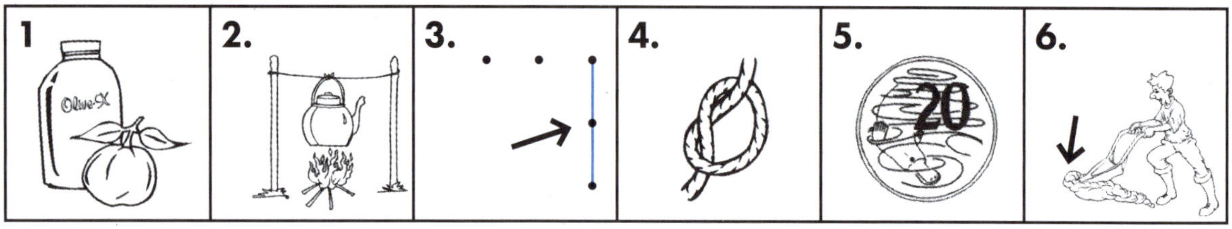

oil join soil

B Use the words in the box to fill the space in each sentence.

joint	voice	noise	boy	toy

1. There was a loud ________________ coming from the room.
2. Sophie cuddled her ________________ bear.
3. When he speaks Ethan has a loud ________________.
4. A ________________ and a girl helped us lift the boxes.
5. In the middle of your finger is a ________________.

C Write these words in sentences of your own:

moist ____

point ____

Parent/Teacher Signature Date

Sound patterns, long and short ea

The letters **ea** together are sometimes pronounced as a long **e** sound, as in **bead**. Sometimes **ea** is pronounced as a short **e** sound, as in **ready**.

A The words in the box all contain the letters **ea** as the long **e** sound. Match each word to its picture and write it on the line.

meat **pea** **leaf** **seat** **seal** **tea**

1. 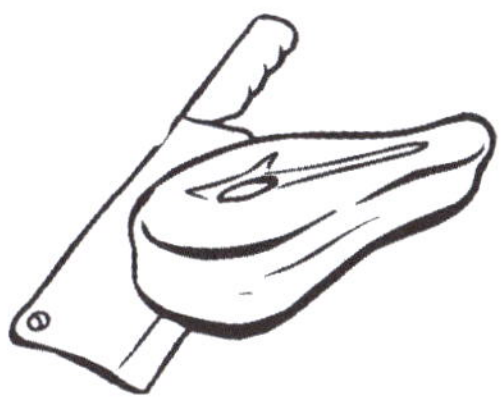 ____________	**2.** 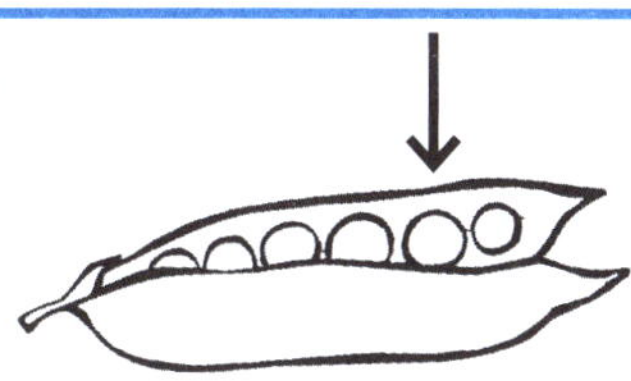 ____________	**3.**  ____________
4. 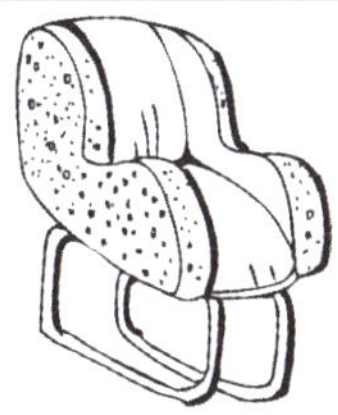 ____________	**5.**  ____________	**6.**  ____________

B The words in the box all contain the letters **ea** as the short **e** sound. Choose the right word to complete each sentence.

head **dead** **bread** **deaf**

1. I spread some butter on the slice of ____________.
2. When he fell he bumped his ____________.
3. If you can't hear you may be ____________.
4. We are sorry that the animal that was hit by the car is ____________.

Parent/Teacher Signature Date

Sound patterns, ow

The letters **ow** sometimes make an **ow** sound, as in **crowd**, and sometimes a long **o** sound, as in **throw**.

A Each word in the box has the **ow** sound as in **crowd**. Write each one under a word that it can be linked to in some way. Draw a picture for each one.

clown	crown	cow	owl	bow	flower

1. bird	**2.** king	**3.** circus
______	______	______
4. milk	**5.** petal	**6.** actor
______	______	______

B All the words below contain **ow** as a long **o** sound. Each one has a smaller word in it. Find and write the smaller word that contains **ow**. Example: narrow, row

1. mower ______
2. below ______
3. snowing ______
4. rowing ______
5. elbow ______
6. shown ______
7. yellow ______
8. owning ______

Parent/Teacher Signature ______ Date ______

Revision

A Write the words from the box under the right headings below.

root	look	broom
book	moon	cook

Long oo (room)	Short oo (look)
______ ______ ______	______ ______ ______

B Add ai or oa in the spaces. Write the words under their headings.

dr___n	c___t	t___l
b___t	sn___l	g___t

ai = long a sound (rain)	oa = long o sound (soap)
______ ______ ______	______ ______ ______

C Add oi or ea in the spaces. Write the words under their headings.

d___d	c___n	s___t
b___l	m___t	h___d

oi (soil)	Long e (peas)	Short e (bread)
______	______	______
______	______	______

Parent/Teacher Signature Date

Test 1

Choose the correct spelling of the word in brackets.
Write the word in the space.

1	My (skule, school) has five teachers.	1
2	Oliver swept the room with a (broom, brum).	2
3	I think it will (rane, rain) today.	3
4	Alicia drew a (train, trian) in her book.	4
5	As it was so cold I wore a (coat, cote).	5
6	My father bought a (lowf, loaf) of bread.	6
7	We will (boyl, boil) the water for a hot drink.	7
8	A five-cent piece is a small (coin, coyn).	8
9	I sat down on the (seat, seet).	9
10	I found a pretty coloured (leaf, leef) on the tree.	10
11	He cut the lawn with a (mouer, mower).	11
12	The (clown, cloun) at the circus made us laugh.	12

Total correct ______ / 12

Parent/Teacher Signature Date

Test 2

The underlined word is spelled wrongly. Write it correctly in the space.

1	I cut some wud to light a fire.	1
2	I ate my cereal with a spune.	2
3	We are going to piant the house blue.	3
4	There was a big snale in the garden.	4
5	On the farm I saw a gote with horns.	5
6	Cork will flote on water.	6
7	I have a new toi to play with.	7
8	There was a loud noyse coming from the room.	8
9	I like to drink a cup of tee.	9
10	Jack tripped and bumped his hed.	10
11	I heard an oul hoot last night.	11
12	The queen wore a croun on her head.	12

Total correct ______ / 12

Parent/Teacher Signature   Date

UNIT 46

Double consonants

Many words contain double consonants, as in **riddle** and **chill**.

A Add a set of double letters from the box to make a word that fits each picture below.

ll **mm** **tt** **bb** **gg** **pp**

1.	2.	3.
 she_____	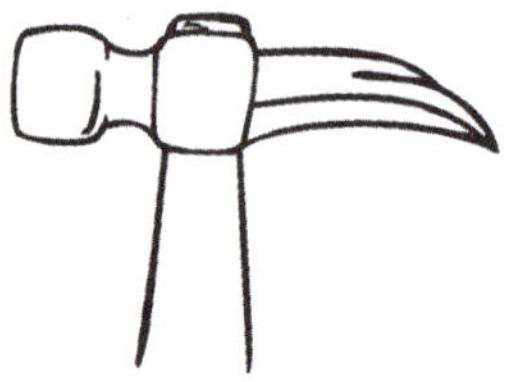 ha_____er	 e_____
4.  pu_____y	5.  ki_____en	6.  ra_____it

B Write each word from the box in the correct space below.

ribbon **swimmer** **jetty**
dinner **happy** **fell**

1. The ship unloaded its cargo at the _______________.
2. We saw a _______________ in the water.
3. Mia tied a blue _______________ in her hair.
4. The boy tripped and _______________ down.
5. I am _______________ you can come.
6. After eating _______________ we had a sleep.

Parent/Teacher Signature Date

Double consonants 2

Many words contain double consonants, as in **riddle** and **chill**.

A Add a set of double letters from the box to complete each word below.

tt	pp	ss	ll	rr	nn

1.  sli_____er	**2.**  bu_____on	**3.** 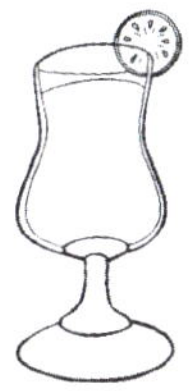 gla_____
4.  ba_____oon	**5.**  che_____y	**6.**  ke_____el

B Add a word from the box to fill the spaces in the sentences below.

off	**small**	**letter**
pillow	**butter**	**middle**

1. I put a dot in the ________________ of the circle.
2. The ________________ on my bed is soft.
3. Lachlan fell ________________ the table and hurt himself.
4. I wrote a ________________ to my penfriend.
5. A mouse is ________________ but an elelphant is large.
6. I spread the ________________ on the bread.

Parent/Teacher Signature   Date

UNIT 48

Word building, word pieces

A Join the word pieces and draw a picture to match.

1. tr + ain ____________	**2.** br + ead ____________	**3.** fl + ag ____________
4. dr + um ____________	**5.** bl + anket ____________	**6.** cr + icket ____________

B Join a word piece in Box B to a word piece in Box A to make a word that matches the picture.

Box A	**Box B**
1. tee	ain
2. f	ape
3. ch	inger
4. cr	oke
5. gr	own
6. sm	th

1. 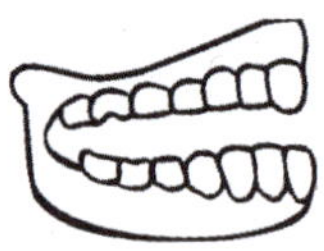 ____________

2. 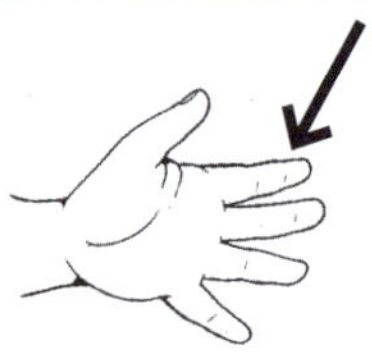 ____________

3. 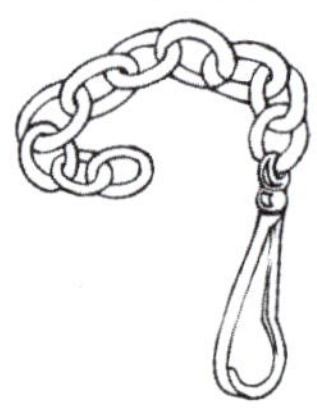 ____________

4.  ____________

5.  ____________

6.  ____________

Parent/Teacher Signature Date

Word building, codes

A Look at the symbol for each letter. Work out what each of the eight words is and write them on the lines below.

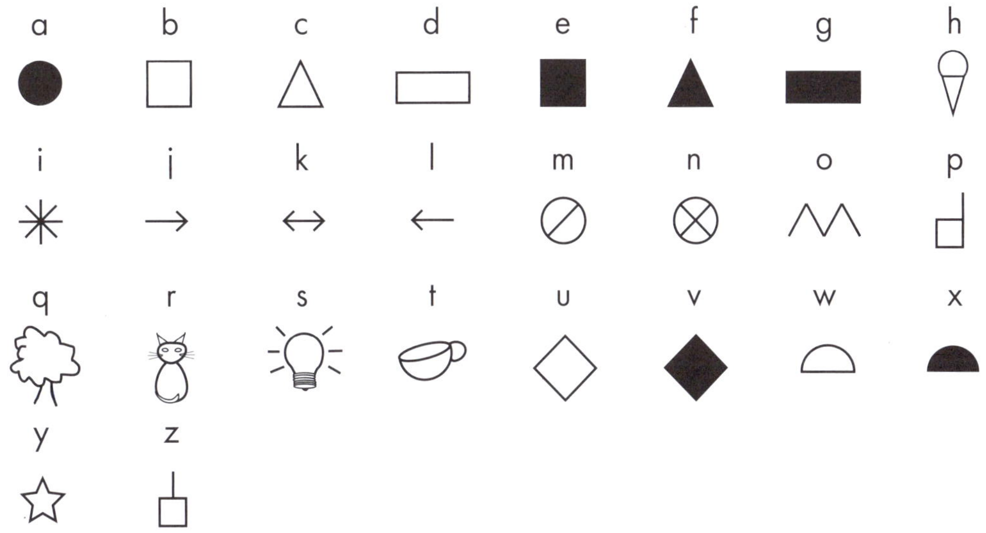

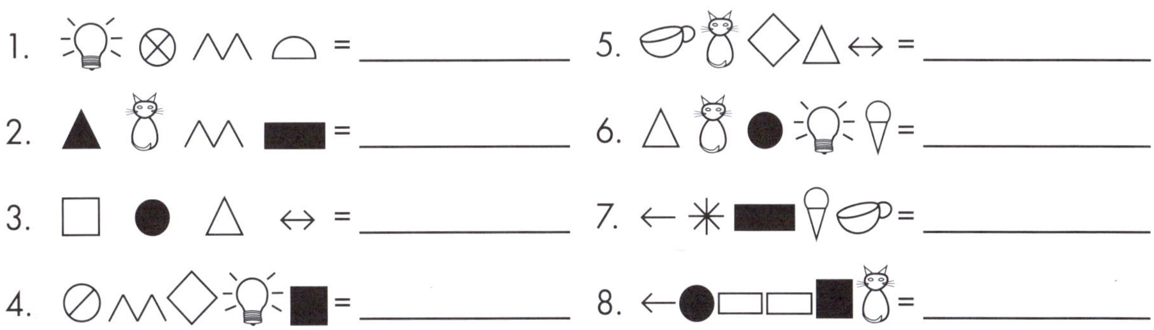

B Work out the names of the creatures by using the code.

f	t	d
x	a	g
c	w	o

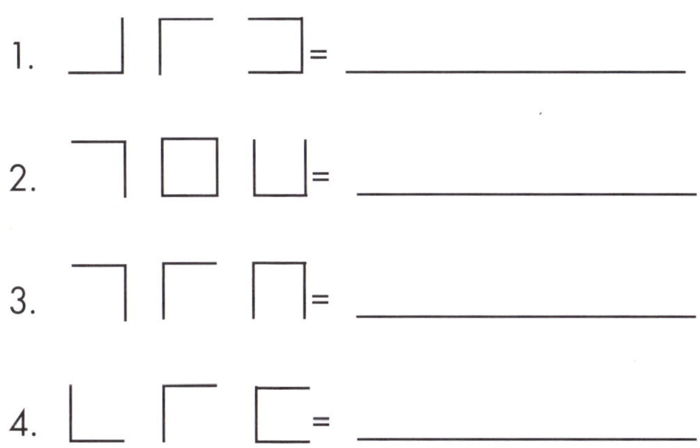

Parent/Teacher Signature   Date

UNIT 50

Revision

A Add double letters to the words in the box. Then write the words under their headings below.

bu___erfly	sa___le	le___er	ra___it
la___er	be___y	ru___er	che___y

bb	tt	rr	dd
________	________	________	________
________	________	________	________

B Join the word pieces to make a complete word. Draw a picture for each one.

1. gl + ove ________	**2.** w + atch ________	**3.** bott + le ________
4. gar + den ________	**5.** chick + en ________	**6.** parr + ot ________

Parent/Teacher Signature Date

Test

Choose the correct spelling of the word in brackets. Write it in the space.

1	I blew up the red (baloon, balloon).	1
2	I saw a (rabbit, rabit) in the garden.	2
3	I helped the teacher (carry, cary) the books.	3
4	Dad boiled the water in the (ketle, kettle).	4
5	Our cat has a new fluffy (kitten, kiten).	5
6	Jack rang the (bel, bell).	6
7	The dog is in the (kenell, kennel).	7
8	I ate the sweet (cherry, chery).	8
9	Our hens lay lots of (eggs, egs).	9
10	At the beach I found a (shel, shell).	10
11	I filled the empty (botle, bottle) with water.	11
12	We put the (sadle, saddle) on the horse.	12

Total correct ______
12

Parent/Teacher Signature Date

Contractions

Contractions are shortened words. Often we join two words and shorten the second word by leaving out letters. We put an apostrophe to show where we have left out a letter or letters.
Example: can + not = can't

A Match each contraction to the words below. Write them on the lines.

you're	I'll	I'm
it's	isn't	don't

1. I am ____________
2. I will ____________
3. you are ____________
4. is not ____________
5. do not ____________
6. it is ____________

B Choose a contraction from the box to replace the words in the brackets.

we're
can't
we'll
aren't
you'll
doesn't

1. If we run quickly (we will) ____________ catch the bus.
2. I think (we are) ____________ going to be late.
3. Mike (does not) ____________ want to come to my party.
4. I just (can not) ____________ find my lost watch.
5. They (are not) ____________ allowed to come with us.
6. If you hurry (you will) ____________ win the race.

Parent/Teacher Signature Date

Anagrams

Anagrams are words that have exactly the same letters but in a different order. Example: pea, ape

A Circle the two words in each box that have exactly the same letters. Draw a picture for one word in each box.

1.	2.	3.
tin ram war arm	spot vase spit post	rain turn runt root
4.	**5.**	**6.**
tear care bear bare	bowl blow blew blot	mart tart part trap

B Rearrange the letters of each word in the box to make another word that matches the pictures below.

grin	**ten**	**rats**
low	**sore**	**lump**

1.	2.	3.
 ____________	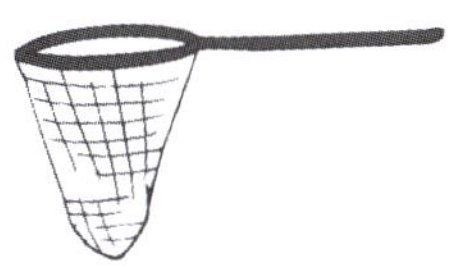 ____________	 ____________
4.	**5.**	**6.**
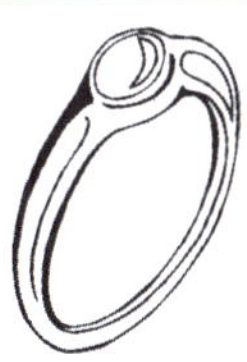 ____________	 ____________	 ____________

Parent/Teacher Signature   Date

UNIT 54

Word search

In the grid, find and colour all the names of creatures.
Use red for mammals. Use blue for birds. Use yellow for insects.
Write the words under their headings below.

e	m	u	b	d
c	o	w	e	o
f	l	y	e	g
a	n	t	x	p
c	a	t	x	i
d	u	c	k	g
w	a	s	p	x
c	r	o	w	x
s	w	a	n	x

Mammals	**Birds**	**Insects**
____________	____________	____________
____________	____________	____________
____________	____________	____________
____________	____________	____________

Parent/Teacher Signature Date

Sound patterns, ou

The letters **ou** can be pronounced in different ways for different words. Sometimes **ou** is sounded as an **ow** sound, as in **ground**. Sometimes **ou** is a long **oo** sound, as in **group**. The letters **ou** can also be a short **u** sound, as in **touch**.

A Choose the correct **ou** sounding word to complete each sentence. Draw a picture for each one.

house **soup** **mountain** **cloud** **mouse** **rough**

1. I had tomato ______________ for lunch.	**2.** The tiny ______________ ate the cheese.	**3.** We saw snow at the top of the ______________.
4. Our ______________ is yellow with a red roof.	**5.** The large ______________ dropped rain down on us.	**6.** The tree bark was very ______________.

B Add an **ou** word from the box to complete each sentence.

south **double** **sour** **young** **round**

1. The opposite of north is ______________________.
2. The opposite of single is ______________________.
3. The opposite of old is ______________________.
4. The opposite of sweet is ______________________.
5. The opposite of square is ______________________.

Parent/Teacher Signature Date

UNIT 56

Sound patterns, ch and sh

Consonants (letters that are not vowels) form a new sound when they are together. The letters ch together are sounded as in **chat**. The letters sh together are sounded as in **shut**. These sound patterns are often at the beginning of a word.

A Sort the words beneath the pictures under the headings below.

 chicken	 church	 sheep	 shed
 shell	 shoe	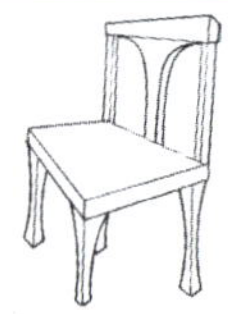 chair	 cherry

ch sound (chat) | **sh sound (shut)**

_______________ _______________ _______________ _______________

_______________ _______________ _______________ _______________

B Unjumble the letters to make a word that begins with the letters sh. The first one has been done for you.

1. hose *shoe* ___________ 2. flesh ___________ 3. posh ___________

4. hares ___________ 5. hooks ___________ 6. hips ___________

Parent/Teacher Signature Date

Sound patterns, ch, sh and ck

The letters **ch** and **sh** form a new sound when they are together. They can be at the beginning or ending of a word, and sometimes in the middle. The letters **ck** together are sounded as in **rock** (the **c** is silent). They are always at the end or middle of a word.

A Sort the words beneath the pictures under the headings below.

 peach	 duck	 watch
 cricket	 witch	 fish
 clock	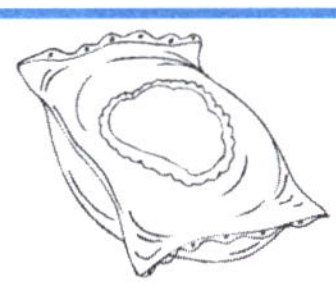 cushion	 bush

ch (much)	**sh (wish)**	**ck (rock)**
______	______	______
______	______	______
______	______	______

B The underlined words contain the letters **ch**, **sh** or **ck**. After each sentence write Yes or No.

1. If you do not have any money you are rich. ______
2. If you are well you are sick. ______
3. You should wash your hands before touching food. ______

Parent/Teacher Signature Date

UNIT 58

Consonant blends 1

Consonant blends are groups of two or more consonants (letters that are not vowels) that are often together.

A Complete each word by adding the blends in the box to the word endings below.

cl	br	bl	fl	dr	cr

1.  ____________aze	**2.**  ____________idge	**3.**  ____________aw
4.  ____________ab	**5.**  ____________ess	**6.**  ____________ower

B Add a word ending from the box to the consonant blends below to complete each word. Draw a picture for each one.

um	own	ag	oom	og	ock

1. fl____________	**2.** fr____________	**3.** dr____________
4. cr____________	**5.** cl____________	**6.** br____________

Parent/Teacher Signature Date

Consonant blends 2

Consonant blends are groups of two or more letters that are often together.

A Use a consonant blend from the box to complete each word below.

gr	pr	cr	sp	sc	pl

1.  _______ider	**2.**  _______ape	**3.**  _______anet
4.  _______am	**5.**  _______arecrow	**6.**  _______ate

B Add a word piece from the box to complete each word. Draw a picture for each one.

oon	ail	ipper	tr	ar	an

1. sn_______	**2.** sp_______	**3.** sw_______
4. _______ain	**5.** st_______	**6.** sl_______

Parent/Teacher Signature Date

Hard and soft g and c

A The letter g can be pronounced as a hard g, as in **golf** and **dug**, or as a soft g, as in **germ** and **gym**.

Write each word from the box under its correct picture.

goat	cage	flag	orange	page	frog

1.  ____________	**2.**  ____________	**3.** 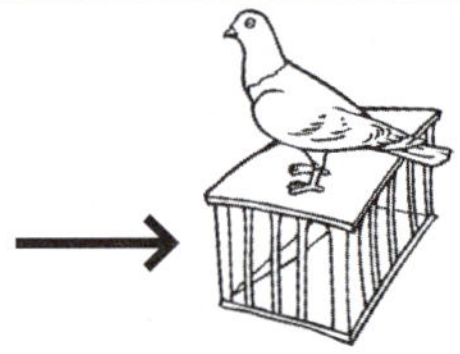 ____________
4.  ____________	**5.**  ____________	**6.**  ____________

B The letter c can be pronounced as a hard c, as in **cost** and **curve** (like a k sound), or it can be a soft c, as in **peace** and **cease** (like an s sound).

Write each word from the box under its correct picture.

sauce	card	cake	fence	cup	circle

1.  ____________	**2.**  ____________	**3.**  ____________
4. 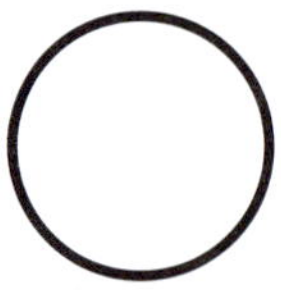 ____________	**5.**  ____________	**6.**  ____________

Parent/Teacher Signature   Date

Revision

A Sort the words beneath the pictures under the headings below.

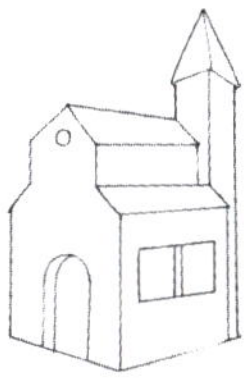 church	 shade	 chair
 shell	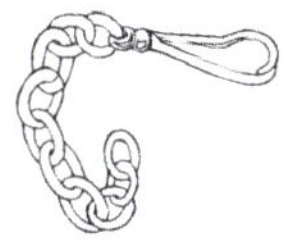 chain	 sheep

ch sound (chat)	**sh sound (shut)**
______________________	______________________
______________________	______________________
______________________	______________________

B Sort the words beneath the pictures under the headings below.

 brush	 duck	 peach
 clock	 fish	 watch

ch (much)	**sh (wish)**	**ck (rock)**
______________	______________	______________
______________	______________	______________

Parent/Teacher Signature Date

Test 1

Choose the correct spelling of the word in brackets. Write it in the space.

1	We had (soup, soop) for dinner.	1
2	The cat chased the small (mouse, mowse).	2
3	The (chain, chane) was made of steel.	3
4	I sat in the (shair, chair).	4
5	A (duk, duck) can quack.	5
6	A large (bush, buch) is in our yard.	6
7	We crossed over the long (brige, bridge).	7
8	Our (clock, clok) is five minutes fast.	8
9	The boys yelled to (skare, scare) him.	9
10	I ate my soup with a (spun, spoon).	10
11	The bird is in the (caje, cage).	11
12	The kangaroo jumped the (fence, fense).	12

Total correct ______
12

Parent/Teacher Signature   Date

Test 2

The underlined word is spelled wrongly. Write it correctly in the space.

1	We played on the sports grownd.	1
2	Tom is old but Mike is yung.	2
3	I lost one of my shus at the picnic.	3
4	The hen had ten shickens.	4
5	I like to play criket.	5
6	I always lok the classroom door.	6
7	Lots of glowers grow in the garden.	7
8	The circus cloun made me laugh.	8
9	I like to scate on the ice.	9
10	We took the trane to Sydney.	10
11	What paje in the book are we up to?	11
12	I filled my kup with hot cocoa.	12

Total correct ______ / 12

Parent/Teacher Signature Date

UNIT 64

Word families 1

Many words use the same letter patterns, as in **bone** and **cone.** These words are part of the same word family. Sometimes the words sound the same and sometimes they are pronounced differently, as in **lone, gone** and **honey.**

A Use the words from the box to complete each sentence below.

bill	hill	fill	kill	pill	gill

1. A duck has a ______________.
2. I will ______________ the bottle with water.
3. The doctor gave the lady a ______________.
4. The cat tried to ______________ a mouse.
5. We were tired after we had climbed the ______________.
6. A fish breathes through a ______________.

B Circle the word that matches the picture.

1.

keep sheep weep

2.

hive dive five

3.

3. rock sock lock

4.

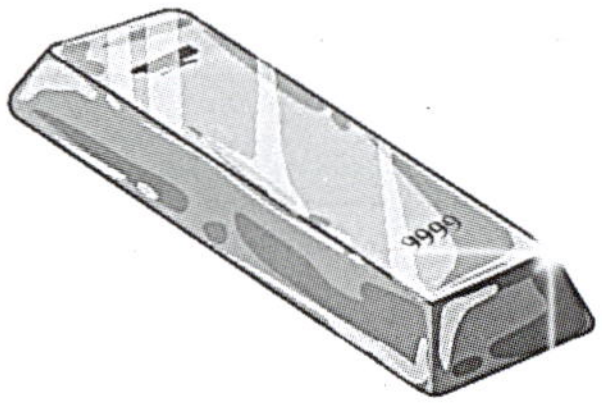

gold sold told

5.

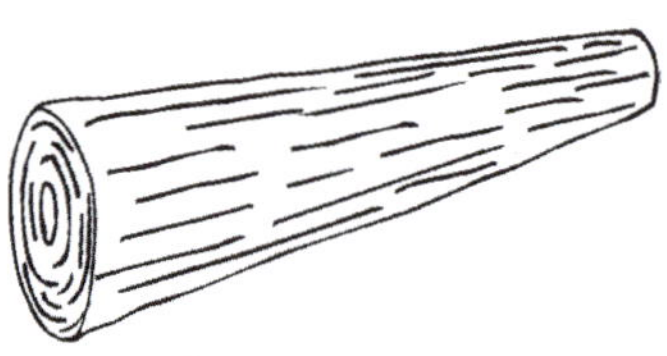

food wood good

6.

row cow slow

Parent/Teacher Signature Date

Word families 2

Many words use the same letter patterns, as in **bone** and **cone**. These words are part of the same word family. Remember, the words don't always sound the same.

A Complete each word below using a letter pattern from the box to match the picture.

one **ice** **eat** **ead** **eer** **est**

1. d________ 
4. n________ 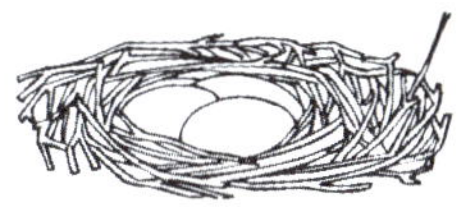
2. br________ 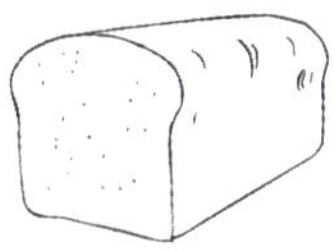
5. c________ 
3. m________ 
6. wh________ 

B Find words in the box that end in **ew**. Use each word in the correct sentence below.

flewscrewdrewsewfewstew

1. My Dad cooked a ______________ for tea.
2. The bird ______________ up into the tree.
3. There were only a ______________ lollies left in the jar.
4. Jack began to ______________ the patch on the cloth.
5. The carpenter will ______________ the pieces of wood together.
6. Brooke ______________ a picture of a dinosaur.

Parent/Teacher Signature   Date

UNIT 66

Word families 3

Many words use the same letter patterns, as in **bone** and **cone**, and are part of the same word family. Remember, the words don't always sound the same.

A Use a word pattern from the box to complete each word below.

ail	**ake**	**eal**	**eel**	**atch**	**ack**

1.  wh__________	**2.**  s__________	**3.**  sn__________
4.  c__________	**5.**  s__________	**6.**  m__________

B Match each word in the box to its family below and write it on the line.

boss	**five**	**cent**	**rose**	**luck**	**seat**

1. meat, heat, beat, __________
2. duck, suck, truck, __________
3. cross, moss, loss, __________
4. close, hose, those, __________
5. bent, tent, lent, __________
6. live, river, hive, __________

Parent/Teacher Signature Date

Word families 4

Many words use the same letter patterns, as in **bone** and **cone**, and are part of the same word family. Remember, the words don't always sound the same.

A Write a word from the box beside its pair below.

wave	**catch**	**late**
paw	**seal**	**read**

1. gate ____________
2. brave ____________
3. jaw ____________
4. meal ____________
5. head ____________
6. match ____________

B Copy each sentence using the correct word from the brackets.

1. The dog licked its (paw, saw).

____

2. We get wool from (sleep, sheep).

____

3. The cat chased the (mice, nice).

____

4. I live in a (sheet, street).

____

5. She wore a (mask, flask) over her face.

____

6. It was a very (warm, harm) day.

____

Parent/Teacher Signature   Date

UNIT 68

Revision

A Group the words in the box under the letter patterns below.

side	**mice**	**screw**
drew	**hide**	**drift**
nice	**lift**	**wide**
gift	**flew**	**lice**

ew	ice	ide	ift
______	______	______	______
______	______	______	______
______	______	______	______

B Find the two words in each row that contain the same letter pattern and write them on the lines.

1.	swell	deep	shell	scarf	______	______
2.	slow	flow	suck	frost	______	______
3.	gave	frock	gift	have	______	______
4.	bend	farm	harm	tide	______	______
5.	boot	corn	duck	horn	______	______
6.	bone	gold	slow	cone	______	______

C Find the word pairs in the box and write them on the lines below.

heat **bash** **seat** **fill** **head** **cash** **kill** **read**

1.______ 2.______ 3.______ 4.______

______ ______ ______ ______

Parent/Teacher Signature Date

Test

Choose the correct spelling of the word in brackets.
Write it in the space.

1	I wore a warm (cote, coat) to school.	1
2	This desk is made of (steel, stele).	2
3	I am going to (baik, bake) a cake.	3
4	The dog chewed the (bown, bone).	4
5	The farmer planted a lot of (corn, curn).	5
6	Bees live in a (hyve, hive).	6
7	A snail is a (pest, peast) in the garden.	7
8	I ate the (croust, crust) of the bread.	8
9	We saw a (gote, goat) at the farm.	9
10	The (clock, clok) belongs to my friend.	10
11	We had a swim in the (pool, puul).	11
12	I rowed the (bowt, boat) across the river.	12

Total correct ______ / 12

Parent/Teacher Signature   Date

UNIT 70

Problem words

For many people, some words are often hard to spell.

A Circle the correct spelling of each word.

1. Do you (lick, like) pizzas?
2. Did you see (wich, which) way she went?
3. Cooper came (first, frist) in the race.
4. I was (gust, just) going inside when the rain began.
5. Is Riley going to (cum, come) to the party?
6. Do you know where (they, thay) are?

B Use a word from the box to complete each sentence below.

where	down	animal	two	house	new

1. Our new ________________ has a tile roof.
2. Do you know ________________ she has gone?
3. A platypus is a very strange ________________.
4. I bought a pair of ________________ shoes today.
5. He tripped and fell ________________ the hole.
6. There are ________________ new boys in our class.

C Find the six words that are cramped up. Write them in the spaces.

saidlookbeentheirmadeword

1.________________ 2.________________ 3.________________

4.________________ 5.________________ 6.________________

Parent/Teacher Signature Date

Changing meaning by changing letters

Many words look almost the same but they have one letter that is different and they have different meanings.

A Change one letter of each word to make a word that matches each picture.

1.  cut ____________	**4.**  bell ____________	**7.** 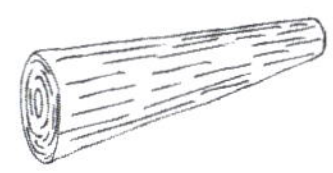 wool ____________
2.  peg ____________	**5.** 10 tea ____________	**8.** 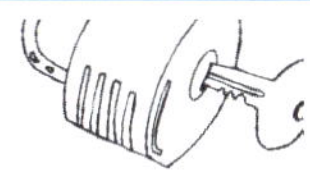 look ____________
3.  hope ____________	**6.**  fail ____________	**9.**  brick ____________

B Change a letter to make a word that fits the meaning.

1. dear ____________ large animal with antlers
2. sail ____________ back part of an animal
3. chain ____________ we sit on it
4. prim ____________ baby carriage
5. park ____________ noise of a dog
6. block ____________ time piece

Parent/Teacher Signature Date

Word search

In the grid, find the words and colour in the boxes. Use red for words that are numbers. Use blue for words that are colours. Use orange for words that are things we eat.

Then write the words under their headings below.

a	p	i	e	b	c
p	r	e	d	l	a
p	t	w	o	u	k
l	s	i	x	e	e
e	m	i	l	k	o
f	o	u	r	x	n
g	r	e	e	n	e
y	e	l	l	o	w

Numbers	Colours	Things we eat
______	______	______
______	______	______
______	______	______
______	______	______

Parent/Teacher Signature Date

Review

A Group the words in the box under the letter patterns below.

five	smoke	bone	cake
me	take	he	kite

Long a (bake)	Long e (she)	Long i (pie)	Long o (nose)
________	________	________	________
________	________	________	________

B Write the words from the box under the headings below.

seal	took	spoon	bread
broom	dead	meat	book

Long oo (room)	Short oo (look)	Short e (head)	Long e (beak)
________	________	________	________
________	________	________	________

C Add ch, sh or ck in each space to match the picture.

1.  pea________	2. 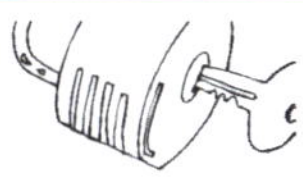 lo________	3.  fi________
4.  bru________	5.  wat________	6.  du________

Parent/Teacher Signature　　　　　　　　Date

Test 1

Choose the correct spelling of the word in brackets.
Write it in the space.

1	It could (rain, rane) today.	1
2	I tore out the (paje, page) in the book.	2
3	At the beach we saw a (wale, whale).	3
4	I blew out the (candel, candle) on the cake.	4
5	Mia wore a blue (dres, dress) to school.	5
6	I like to eat a meat (pye, pie).	6
7	We get (milk, milck) from cows.	7
8	I hit the (nale, nail) with the hammer.	8
9	I stuck a (stamp, stamf) on the letter.	9
10	The dog chewed the (bown, bone)	10
11	The colour of this paper is (blue, blu).	11
12	A (duck, duk) can swim well.	12

Total correct ________
12

Parent/Teacher Signature Date

Test 2

The underlined word is spelled wrongly. Write it correctly in the space.

1	I grow flowers in my <u>gardin</u>.	1
2	The fisherman caught a <u>shaak</u>.	2
3	The parrot sat on a <u>pirch</u> in a cage.	3
4	I am learning many new <u>werds</u>.	4
5	I cut off the <u>krust</u> of the loaf of bread.	5
6	We always <u>lok</u> our house at night.	6
7	Jack has hurt his right <u>fut</u>.	7
8	He is the <u>therd</u> person today to forget his lunch.	8
9	I drew a <u>cercle</u> in my book.	9
10	I washed my face with <u>sope</u>.	10
11	I sat and rested on the <u>seet</u>.	11
12	We like to have tomato <u>supe</u> for lunch.	12

Total correct ______ / 12

Parent/Teacher Signature   Date

Test 3

Choose the correct spelling of the word in brackets. Write it in the space.

1	The dog has a sore (tale, tail).	1
2	Next (week, weak) we are going on an excursion.	2
3	Oliver (new, knew) the answer to the question.	3
4	The axeman cut the (wood, would).	4
5	We went to the (see, sea) for a holiday.	5
6	The prisoner was kept in a (sell, cell).	6
7	My (shoelace, shulace) was undone.	7
8	I have a painful (tuthacke, toothache).	8
9	(I'll, Isle) come when he lets me.	9
10	I dont think (its, it's) time to go.	10
11	I put the cereal in the (bowl, blow).	11
12	We saw a (rats, star) twinkling in the sky.	12

Total correct ______ / 12

Parent/Teacher Signature   Date

Useful Words

able
above
after
again
along
among
angry
animal
any
axe
baby
bare
bead
bean
bear
been
begin
better
brake
bread
build
bunch
butter
candle
care
catch
caught
chair
chalk
claw
clean
climb
coal
colour
comb
corner
cotton
cover
crust
cube
dawn
death
dinner
does
done
dream
each
earn
eat
eggs
eight
every
facing
fall
feel
fence
fight
fleet
flesh
flies
flying
fowl
free
fright
gain
garden
gas
girl
glove
goat
goose
grapes
grate
ground
grow
hammer
handle
happy
hawk
head
heel
help
here
hunger
ice
indeed
iron
jacket
jelly
juice
jumped
just
keep
kick
kitten
knife
know
lace
ladder
lawn
lead
leaf
leak
letter
limb
lion
load
loaf
loan
love
low
made
main
make
making
manner
meal
middle
mother
mountain
mouse
mouth
nail
nasty
nearly
neat
needle
none
not
number
oak
oats
offer
only
orange
order
our
oven
own
pair
pale
paw
peace
peach
pear
piece
please
pony
pretty
pride
prize
pudding
queen
race
rain
raw
read
ribbon
riding
right
river
road
roar
roast
roll
rope
rough
running
sail
salt
school
seam
seek
seen
shadow
shell
shooting
smile
some
stalk
steamer
store
struck
sweet
table
tail
tale
tall
thumb
tight
toe
too
truth
tune
two
under
upper
urn
want
watch
whale
with
yard
year

WINK: Words I Need to Know

For many people, some words are often hard to spell. Record words you are having difficulty with on this page.

Word	Word	Word

Some Tips for Learning to Spell

Spelling can seem really hard sometimes. There are so many different words and rules for spelling them. Follow these tips to help you learn and improve your spelling.

- ★ When you read a story you might notice that some words contain the same letter patterns. Look at this story:

  > One morning a tall boy looked in a box trying to find a rubber ball and a soft stuffed toy fox he wanted to play with out on the grass, but all he could find was an old brass horn.

  Can you see words that have the same letters or sounds? Remembering these pattterns can help you become a better speller.
- ★ When you read a story you find many interesting words. Think about what makes these words a little different from others. For example, think of the words **queue** and **hijinks**. How do they seem different from other words?
- ★ Always try to say words correctly. It is a **river**, not a **riva**, and a **teacher**, not a **teacha**. We go **swimming**, not **swimmen**, and we go **climbing** trees, not **climen** trees.
- ★ When you are writing a story and don't really know how to spell a word, write the first letter and then put a dash. Ask your teacher or parents to help you spell it, or use a dictionary to check and write the word yourself. For example, you might write: Jack was chased by the g______. And later you can complete your sentence:
  Jack was chased by the giant.
- ★ For words that give you trouble, write them on the WINK page so you will remember the words you need to know. This can be your own little spelling dictionary.
- ★ If the word tricks you again, LOOK at the word, COVER it up and try to WRITE it from memory. Then CHECK it. Keep doing this until you are really sure how to spell the word.
- ★ The best tip is to really try hard so you become tops at spelling. Read as much as you can and take care when you write a story that the words you write are correct.

Assessment

	T1	T2	T3	T4
★ Demonstrates an awareness of the need for correct spelling.				
★ Can describe the strategies used to achieve correct spelling in own writing.				
★ Can describe and discuss own knowledge of spelling.				
★ Is able to categorise words by sound sequence or letter pattern.				
★ Articulates individual words clearly and listens to and recognises the sounds in words.				
★ Uses familiar sound and visual patterns to remember the spelling of words.				
★ Proofreads own writing and corrects errors continually by circling them.				
★ Is prepared to source the correct spelling of difficult or unknown words.				
★ Checks spelling with reliable sources such as wall charts or simple dictionaries.				
★ Applies simple spelling guides and strategies.				
★ Uses memory keys or mnemonics to remember difficult words.				
★ Confidently uses the LOOK, COVER, WRITE, CHECK method to remember the spelling of new or difficult words.				

Comments

Areas of strength: ______________________________

____

Areas of difficulty: ______________________________

____

Future needs or steps to be undertaken: ______________________________

____

____

Parent/Teacher Signature ______________________________ Date ____________

Glossary of Terms

anagram
The letters of a *word* or words that can make another word when jumbled up.
Example: **fowl** and **wolf**.

base word
A *word* to which *prefixes* and *suffixes* can be added. Example: **obey** (base word) + **dis** (prefix) = **disobey** + **ed** (suffix) = **disobeyed**

compound word
A *word* made up of two or more smaller words, often developing first as a hyphenated word.
Example: **butter** + **fly** = **butterfly**

consonant
A letter in which the air is in some way impeded when pronounced. There are 21 consonants in the alphabet, all the letters that are not *vowels*.

consonant blend
When two or more *consonants* come together to blend a sound. Examples: **stick**, **sky**, **brown**, **straw**
Consonant blends may be initial blends (**frog**), medial (middle) blends (**blister**), or final blends (**stamp**).

contraction
A *word* in which one or more letters have been omitted and in their place an apostrophe inserted. Examples: **I would** becomes **I'd; is not** becomes **isn't**

digraph
A combination of letters that represents a single sound. There are *consonant* digraphs and *vowel* digraphs. Common consonant digraphs include **sh**, **ch**, **th** and **wh**. (Consonant digraphs at the beginning of a word are called an onset; vowel digraphs are also called diphthongs.)

double consonant
Two consonants that occur in a word; sometimes they occur when we add a suffix.
Examples: **rabbit; run**, **running**

homophone
A word that is pronounced the same as another word, but each word has a different spelling and a different meaning (a type of *homonym*).
Examples: **bear** (a furry animal) and **bare** (naked) **sure** (certain) and **shore** (coastline)

letter pattern
A letter sequence that functions as a unit and is related to a consistent category of sound.
Example: **one** = **bone**, **cone**, **tone**

long vowel
The sound of a *vowel* (**a**, **e**, **i**, **o**, **u**) that says its letter name, or is an *r-influenced vowel*.
Examples: **same**, **bacon**, **far**, **concrete**, **fever**, **fine**, **rival**, **fir**, **cone**, **robot**, **core**, **cute**, **student**, **purr**

phonics
The systematic relationship between letters and sounds.

plural
More than one. Most words make their plurals by adding an **s**. However, there are other ways to make the plurals of words. Examples: **girl**, **girls**; **watch**, **watches**; **city**, **cities**; **piano**, **pianos**; **knife**, **knives**; **tooth**, **teeth**; **mouse**, **mice**

r-influenced vowel
A *vowel* sound that is determined by the letter **r** following it. Example: The **a** in **far** is a *long vowel* sound but the **a** in **fad** is a *short vowel* sound.

short vowel
The sound of a *vowel* (**a**, **e**, **i**, **o** and **u**) that is clipped — a short sound. It is sometimes said short vowel sounds are the "baby" sounds.
Examples: **bat**, **bet**, **bit**, **bottle**, **but**

suffix
A group of letters added to the end of a *word* to alter its part of speech or meaning. Spelling changes are often needed.
Examples: **tie** + **ed** = **tied**; **watch** + **ed** = **watched**; **ride** + **ing** = **riding**; **watch** + **ing** = **watching**; **beauty** + **ful** = **beautiful**

syllable
A sound unit that includes only one sounded *vowel*. The vowel may be preceded or followed by several *consonants*. Words can be divided into their syllables. This is a useful spelling technique.
Example: **development** = **de** / **vel** / **op** / **ment**

vowel
A letter in which the air passes through the mouth without obstruction when pronounced. The letters **a**, **e**, **i**, **o** and **u** are vowels. Note: **y** does the work of the vowels **i** and **e** in words such as **cry** (long **i**), **mystery** (short **i**) and **weary** (long **e**).

word
A unit of meaning. A word may be a simple *syllable* or a combination of syllables. A word may contain smaller units of meaning within it.

word building
Adding a new letter group to a word, such as a *suffix*, to build a more complex word.

word family
A group of words that use the same letter pattern, though they do not necessarily sound the same.
Examples: **bone, cone, gone, honey, lone, money, stone, tone**

Answers, Class 2

Unit 1
A
1. grapes
2. play
3. bake
4. stay
5. train
6. snail

B
1. whale
2. nail
3. rain
4. mail
5. spade
6. shave

Unit 2
A
1. flag
2. lamb
3. axe
4. rat
5. hat
6. ant

B
1. quack
2. stamp
3. sand
4. candle

Unit 3
A
1. week
2. sheet
3. he
4. me
5. she
6. keep

B
1. teeth
2. peel
3. bench
4. bean

Unit 4
A
1. wet
2. pen
3. tent
4. cents
5. ten
6. rest

B
bed
dress
shed
nest
egg
shell

Unit 5
A
1. kite
2. five
3. mice
4. pine
5. eye
6. vine

B
1. Yes
2. Yes
3. No
4. Yes
5. No
6. Yes

Unit 6
A
1. king
2. dish
3. swim
4. whip
5. chin
6. hill

B
1. fish
2. pig
3. thin
4. milk
5. chick
6. bin

Unit 7 Revision
A
Long a:
page
race
nail
stay
Short a:
glad
mat
hat
flag

B
Long e:
me
she
keep
week
Short e:
best
cent
wet
tent

C
Long i:
nice
sky
kite
fire
Short i:
win
list
chip
thick

Unit 8 Test 1
1. snail
2. rain
3. stamp
4. quack
5. shed
6. weed
7. tent
8. egg
9. kite
10. eye
11. fish
12. chick

Unit 9 Test 2
1. stay
2. nail
3. axe
4. candle
5. week
6. keep
7. shell
8. cents
9. pie
10. mice
11. milk
12. swim

Unit 10
1. cats
2. bikes
3. houses
4. chairs
5. hens
6. tables
7. balls
8. cows

Unit 11
1. peaches
2. bushes
3. brushes
4. churches
5. watches
6. dishes
7. witches
8. bunches

Unit 12
A
1. boxes
2. buses
3. glasses
4. foxes
5. dresses
6. kisses

B
1. guesses
2. hisses
3. classes
4. bosses

Unit 13
A
1. boys
2. keys
3. turkeys
4. monkeys
5. donkeys
6. toys

B
1. mice
2. men
3. teeth
4. children

Unit 14 Revision
A
Singular:
dish
dress
bunch
desk
monkey
box
church
book
Plural:
boxes
guesses
tables
donkeys
matches
turkeys
mice
teeth

B
+ s:
days
trees
gloves
circles
+ es:
bushes
witches
boxes
ditches
Word change:
mice
feet
geese
men

Unit 15 Test
1. cats
2. tables
3. birds
4. peaches
5. dishes
6. bushes
7. buses
8. dresses
9. keys
10. toys
11. mice
12. teeth

Unit 16
A
1. armchair
2. starfish
3. waterfall
4. eggcup
5. butterfly
6. football
7. blackbird
8. shoelace
9. grasshopper
B
1. bathroom
2. bulldog
3. afternoon
4. birthday
5. snowflake
6. pancakes

Unit 17
A
1. goldfish
2. rainbow
3. seaside
4. horseshoe
5. toothpaste
6. necklace
B
1. spaceship
2. strawberry
3. grasshopper
4. newspaper
5. bathroom
6. windmill

Unit 18
A
Across:
1. bat
3. gun
Down:
1. bug
2. ten
B
Across:
1. cap
3. rat
Down:
1. car
2. pot
C
Across:
1. cow
3. tug
Down:
1. cat
2. wig
D
Across:
1. fan
3. tap
Down:
1. fat
2. nap

Unit 19
A
1. nose
2. loaf
3. rose
4. bone
5. soap
6. smoke
B
1. rope
2. toe
3. smoke
4. nose
5. hose
6. home

Unit 20
A
1. fox
2. lollipop
3. rod
4. sock
5. lock
6. clock
B
1. Yes
2. Yes
3. No
4. No
5. Yes
6. Yes

Unit 21
A
1. pure
2. cube
3. tune
4. cute
5. fume
6. cure
B
1. No
2. Yes
3. Yes
4. No
5. No
6. No

Unit 22
A
1. hut
2. truck
3. bus
4. gun
5. bug
6. trunk
B
1. plum
2. bun
3. cup
4. jug

Unit 23
A
1. star
2. farm
3. garden
4. card
5. shark
6. park
B
1. carpet
2. arms
3. bark
4. dark
5. hard
6. shark

Unit 24
A
1. bird
2. worm
3. person
4. turtle

5. dancer
6. circle
B
1. verse
2. perch
3. surf
4. fern
5. birthday
6. circus

Unit 25 Revision
A
Long o:
stone
home
boat
woke
Short o:
stop
clock
shop
lock
B
Long u:
huge
tube
cure
pure
Short u:
lump
crust
plum
luck
C
ar:
card
star
bark
arm
er:
her
herb
fern
germ

Unit 26 Test 1
1. loaf
2. bone
3. clock
4. sock
5. cute
6. huge
7. ducks
8. truck
9. card
10. shark
11. circus
12. fern

Unit 27 Test 2
1. soap
2. smoke
3. lock
4. moth
5. pure
6. student
7. truck
8. trunk
9. garden
10. park
11. shirt
12. term

Unit 28
A
Short words:
in
cat
the
is
of
sit
Long words:
cupboard
kangaroo
helicopter
elephant
aeroplane
holidays
B
1. A bird can fly.
2. My cat is black.
3. We went on a ship.

Unit 29
A
1. jumped
2. washed
3. played
4. pushed
5. sailed
6. cooked
B
1. helped
2. called
3. turned
4. crawled
5. stayed
6. looked

Unit 30
A
1. cooking
2. learning
3. calling
4. sailing
5. pushing
6. mowing

B
1. jumping
2. playing
3. sleeping
4. crawling
5. turning
6. helping

Unit 31
A
1. chopped
2. mopped
3. dropped
4. hopped
5. skipped
6. patted
B
1. stopping
2. wagging
3. tripping
4. rubbing
5. grabbing
6. slipping

Unit 32 Revision
A
Short words:
and
but
if
hit
Medium words:
driver
sailor
house
table
Long words:
aeroplane
helicopter
hippopotamus
beautiful
B
+ ed:
waited
jumped
played
passed
Double last letter + ed:
wagged
stopped
hopped
dragged
C
1. playing
2. stopping
3. helping

Unit 33 Test
1. jumped
2. cooked
3. sailed
4. helped
5. chopped
6. dropped
7. patted
8. rubbed
9. learning
10. calling
11. cooking
12. sleeping

Unit 34
A
1. four
2. sun
3. sail
4. tail
5. meat
6. mail
B
1. to
2. meet
3. week
4. tail
5. buy
6. knew

Unit 35
B
1. bee
2. saw
3. road
4. pear
5. ate
6. knot

Unit 36
A
1. ship
2. egg
3. star
4. pig
5. sun

B
1. tree
2. ring
3. gate
4. bird
5. gold

Unit 37
A
Long oo:
boot
moon
broom
school
Short oo:
book
hook
foot
wood
B
1. brook
2. hood
3. spoon

Unit 38
A
1. train
2. rain
3. tail
4. mail
5. paint
6. snail

B
1. Yes
2. No
3. Yes
4. Yes

Unit 39
A
1. boat
2. soap
3. goat
4. coat
5. loaf
6. road

B
1. Yes
2. Yes
3. Yes
4. No
5. Yes
6. Yes

Unit 40
A
1. oil
2. boil
3. join
4. coil
5. coin
6. soil

B
1. noise
2. toy
3. voice
4. boy
5. joint

Unit 41
A
1. meat
2. pea
3. leaf
4. seat
5. seal
6. tea

B
1. bread
2. head
3. deaf
4. dead

Unit 42
A
1. owl
2. crown
3. clown
4. cow
5. flower
6. bow

B
1. mow, owe
2. low
3. snow, now
4. row
5. bow
6. how, show
7. low
8. own

Unit 43 Revision
A
Long oo:
root
moon
broom
Short oo:
book
look
cook
B
ai:
drain
snail
tail
oa:
boat
coat
goat
C
oi:
boil
coin
Long e:
meat
seat
Short e:
dead
head

Unit 44 Test 1
1. school
2. broom
3. rain
4. train
5. coat
6. loaf
7. boil
8. coin
9. seat
10. leaf
11. mower
12. clown

Unit 45 Test 2
1. wood
2. spoon
3. paint
4. snail
5. goat
6. float
7. toy
8. noise
9. tea
10. head
11. owl
12. crown

Unit 46
A
1. shell
2. hammer
3. egg
4. puppy
5. kitten
6. rabbit

B
1. jetty
2. swimmer
3. ribbon
4. fell
5. happy
6. dinner

Unit 47
A
1. slipper
2. button
3. glass
4. balloon
5. cherry
6. kennel

B
1. middle
2. pillow
3. off
4. letter
5. small
6. butter

Unit 48
A
1. train
2. bread
3. flag
4. drum
5. blanket
6. cricket
B
1. teeth
2. finger
3. chain
4. crown
5. grape
6. smoke

Unit 49
A
1. snow
2. frog
3. back
4. mouse
5. truck
6. crash
7. light
8. ladder
B
1. fox
2. cat
3. cow
4. dog

Unit 50 Revision
A
bb:
rabbit
rubber
tt:
butterfly
letter
rr:
berry
cherry
dd:
saddle
ladder
B
1. glove
2. watch
3. bottle
4. garden
5. chicken
6. parrot

Unit 51 Test
1. balloon
2. rabbit
3. carry
4. kettle
5. kitten
6. bell
7. kennel
8. cherry
9. eggs
10. shell
11. bottle
12. saddle

Unit 52
A
1. I'm
2. I'll
3. you're
4. isn't
5. don't
6. it's
B
1. we'll
2. we're
3. doesn't
4. can't
5. aren't
6. you'll

Unit 53
A
1. arm, ram
2. spot, post
3. turn, runt
4. bear, bare
5. bowl, blow
6. trap, part
B
1. owl
2. net
3. star
4. ring
5. rose
6. plum

Unit 54
Mammals:
cow
dog
pig
cat
Birds:
emu
duck
crow
swan
Insects:
fly
ant
wasp
bee

Unit 55
A
1. soup
2. mouse
3. mountain
4. house
5. cloud
6. rough
B
1. south
2. double
3. young
4. sour
5. round

Unit 56
A
ch:
chicken
church
chair
cherry
sh:
sheep
shed
shell
shoe
B
1. shoe
2. shelf
3. shop
4. share
5. shook
6. ship

Unit 57
A
ch:
peach
witch
watch
sh:
cushion
fish
bush
ck:
cricket
clock
duck
B
1. No
2. No
3. Yes

Unit 58
1. blaze
2. bridge
3. claw
4. crab
5. dress
6. flower
B
1. flag
2. frog
3. drum
4. crown
5. clock
6. broom

Unit 59
A
1. spider
2. grape
3. planet
4. pram
5. scarecrow
6. crate
B
1. snail
2. spoon
3. swan
4. train
5. star
6. slipper

Unit 60
A
1. frog
2. flag
3. cage
4. orange
5. goat
6. page

B
1. cup
2. cake
3. fence
4. circle
5. card
6. sauce

Unit 61 Revision
A
ch:
church
chair
chain
sh:
shade
shell
sheep
B
ch:
peach
watch
sh:
brush
fish
ck:
duck
clock

Unit 62 Test 1
1. soup
2. mouse
3. chain
4. chair
5. duck
6. bush
7. bridge
8. clock
9. scare
10. spoon
11. cage
12. fence

Unit 63 Test 2
1. ground
2. young
3. shoes
4. chickens
5. cricket
6. lock
7. flowers
8. clown
9. skate
10. train
11. page
12. cup

Unit 64
A
1. bill
2. fill
3. pill
4. kill
5. hill
6. gill

B
1. sheep
2. hive
3. sock
4. gold
5. wood
6. cow

Unit 65
A
1. deer
2. bread
3. mice
4. nest
5. cone
6. wheat

B
1. stew
2. flew
3. few
4. sew
5. screw
6. drew

Unit 66
A
1. wheel
2. sack
3. snake
4. catch
5. sail
6. meal

B
1. seat
2. luck
3. boss
4. rose
5. cent
6. five

Unit 67
A
1. late
2. wave
3. paw
4. seal
5. read
6. catch

B
1. paw
2. sheep
3. mice
4. street
5. mask
6. warm

Unit 68 Revision
A
ew:
drew
flew
screw
ice:
nice
mice
lice
ide:
side
hide
wide
ift:
gift
lift
drift
B
1. swell, shell
2. slow, flow
3. gave, have
4. farm, harm
5. corn, horn
6. bone, cone

C
1. heat, seat
2. bash, cash
3. fill, kill
4. head, read

Unit 69 Test
1. coat
2. steel
3. bake
4. bone
5. corn
6. hive
7. pest
8. crust
9. goat
10. clock
11. pool
12. boat

Unit 70
A
1. like
2. which
3. first
4. just
5. come
6. they

B
1. house
2. where
3. animal
4. new
5. down
6. two

C
1. said
2. look
3. been
4. their
5. made
6. word

Unit 71
A
1. cat
2. pig
3. hose
4. ball
5. ten
6. fall
7. wood

8. lock
9. brick

B

1. deer
2. tail
3. chair
4. pram
5. bark
6. clock

Unit 72

Numbers:
four
two
six
one
Colours:
red
green
yellow
blue
Things we eat:
apple
pie
milk
cake

Unit 73 Review

A

Long a:
take
cake
Long e:
me
he
Long i:
five
kite
Long o:
smoke
bone

B

Long oo:
broom
spoon
Short oo:
took
book
Short e:
dead
bread
Long e:
seat
meat

C

1. peach
2. lock
3. fish
4. brush
5. watch
6. duck

Unit 74 Test 1

1. rain
2. page
3. whale
4. candle
5. dress
6. pie
7. milk
8. nail
9. stamp
10. bone
11. blue
12. duck

Unit 75 Test 2

1. garden
2. shark
3. perch
4. words
5. crust
6. lock
7. foot
8. third
9. circle
10. soap
11. seat
12. soup

Unit 76 Test 3

1. tail
2. week
3. knew
4. wood
5. sea
6. cell
7. shoelace
8. toothache
9. I'll
10. it's
11. bowl
12. star